THE GATEFOLD BOOK OF
HARLEY-DAVIDSON

Photographs by Garry Stuart

Text by John Carroll

BROWN BOOKS

Brown Books
255-257 Liverpool Road
London N1 1LX

ISBN: 1 897884 23 0

Printed in Italy

Conceived and produced by Brown Packaging Books Ltd
255-257 Liverpool Road
London N1 1LX

Acknowledgements
The publisher would like to thank the following for the use of their Harley-Davidsons:
Airbrush Willie, Robert Ashman, Battistini's Custom Cycles, Peter Buchly, Chris Butler,
Ron and Wendy Coles, Danny Fransen, Jeremy Griffin, Stuart Hall, Martin Henderson,
Leo Keizer, Lou Marlow, Vince Martin, Mike Morse, Michel Nivarlet, O.I.T., Chris Parry,
Phil Piper, Dale Richardson, Martin Snippert, Gerry Stockwell, Terry Sweeney,
Richard Taylor, Simon Winslow and
Motex Ltd, Shire Park, Warndon, Worcester, England WR4 9FD. Tel. 01905 756883.

Contents

The Making of a Legend

What it's all about; riding customized Harley-Davidsons in the hot August sunshine, listening to the V-twins' off-beat rumble on the wide open road between Deadwood and the annual biker gathering in Sturgis, South Dakota.

Harley and Davidson – two family surnames that together make one of the most recognized motorcycle marques in the world. It has also grown into an American icon, with classic films such as *Easy Rider* and *Electraglide in Blue* helping to further the myth of the Harley. The history of the Harley-Davidson is both long and proud and began modestly in the early years of the twentieth century.

In 1903, two of the Davidson brothers, Arthur and Walter, together with William S. Harley, used their spare time to build a single-cylinder motorcycle that displaced approximately 10 cu in (160 cc). It worked well but lacked hill-climbing ability, so the group built two improved motorcycles in 1904 with the intention of selling them. The Davidson brothers' Aunt Janet pinstriped the finished machines prior to their sale. The company was now in business and production grew exponentially; in 1905 the group made eight motorcycles, in 1906 they produced 50, 150 in 1907 and over 400 in

1908. Their first factory was nothing more than a shed built by the Davidsons' father and it was then that the third Davidson brother, William A., joined the fledgling company. Harley-Davidson filed its incorporation papers in 1907. The company was up and running and would stay under the control of the Harley and Davidson families until 1969 when American Machine and Foundry (AMF) bought them out.

EARLY SUCCESS

The Harley-Davidson company are, of course, famous for their V-twin-engined motorcycles and the first successful one was produced in 1911. It was followed a year later by the 8E, a 45° 61 cu in (1000 cc) V-twin. In 1913, sales of Harley-Davidsons reached a record 12,904 units and the company started to think about exporting

their bikes. They engaged an Englishman, Duncan Watson, to arrange imports and sales in the UK and Europe, but the outbreak of World War I less than a year later meant that exports to Europe ceased and they did not resume again until 1919. On the positive side, the war provided Harley-Davidson with the opportunity to supply the US Army with their motorcycles.

In 1921, Douglas Davidson (no relation) became the first person to exceed 100 mph (161 km/h) on a motorcycle in Britain, and it was on a Harley. He achieved this feat at Brooklands, the legendary English racing circuit, and recorded a speed of 100.76 mph (162.12 km/h). However, the year was not altogether successful for the company as sales were down more than 18,000 on 1920's record high of 28,189, and as a result Harley-Davidson made their first end-of-year loss. One of the reasons for this drop in sales was Ford's mass-produced car, the Model-T, which was selling for almost the same price as a motorbike and sidecar. With approximately 75 per cent of Harley-Davidsons leaving the factory with sidecars, the figures speak for themselves.

Exports did not suffer as badly, however, and the company embarked on an extensive programme to bolster sales around the globe. One employee, Alfred Rich Child, went to Cape Town in South Africa and then rode the full length of the continent on a J Model. He sold 400 motorcycles en route and secured a number of new dealers for the company. Child then went to Japan and spent the next 13 years importing Harley-Davidsons into the country. He also established a licensing agreement with a company called Rikuo to enable Harleys to be made in Japan.

After the 1921 slump, sales began to increase again, aided by the introduction of the first 74 cu in (1200 cc) models. The engine's large capacity made it more suitable for pulling a sidecar and matched engines made by Harley's major rivals Indian Motorcycles from Springfield, Massachusetts. This first 74 was known as an F-head, a term to indicate the position of the inlet and exhaust valves; earlier models were known as IOE (inlet over exhaust).

ENGINE REFINEMENTS

In 1928, a new chapter opened for Harley-Davidson. Not only did they start fitting front brakes to their products for the first time, but they unveiled a new engine. It was a side-valve V-twin that displaced 45 cu in (740 cc). The new model was tagged the D Model, but an unreliable gearbox and clutch and a maximum speed of only 55 mph (88 km/h) produced early teething problems. The model was discontinued for 1929 and returned in 1930 in three guises: the D, DL, and DLD. The different designations referred to the power outputs of the machines – 15, 18.5 and 20 horsepower respectively.

Then came the infamous Wall Street Crash of 1929 and Harley-Davidson were in trouble. Their sales declined over the next year to an all-time low of only 3703 machines. In addition, export sales were affected by the introduction of higher import taxes in Australia and New Zealand. Another American motorcycle manufacturer,

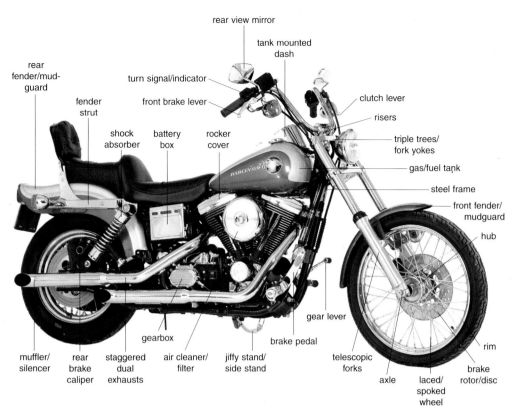

The main components of a Harley-Davidson motorcycle annotated with American and English terms where appropriate.

Excelsior, could not take the pressure and closed in 1931, leaving Indian as Harley's only domestic competitor. Harley-Davidson resorted to desperate measures to attract customers; a wider choice of colours, extra chrome parts, optional accessories, and even an extra wheel.

In 1932, the Milwaukee company unveiled the Servicar, a three-wheeled machine powered by the 45 cu in (740 cc) side-valve engine. It was aimed at small businesses, garages and police departments. Garages used to send their mechanics out on them to breakdowns, small businesses used them as delivery vehicles and policemen handed out parking tickets from them. The first Servicars featured the D Model engine, although the vehicles were later upgraded in line with the solo 45 cu in (740 cc) models. The upgrades included new designations, R and RL models and subsequently WL models. The 80 cu in (1310 cc) flatheads were also introduced in 1936 and designated U Models.

Parallel to the development of the side-valve engine, Harley was developing an overhead-valve engine and this went into production in 1936. It was designated the 61E Model, the 61 equating to its displacement in cubic inches (1000 cc). The engine soon became referred to as the 'Knucklehead' because of the resemblance of the rocker covers to human knuckles. It

was the first Harley to have dry sump lubrication instead of a total loss system The horseshoe-shaped oil tank was located under the seat, the engine was fitted into a double loop frame and a new style of gas tank appeared. It was made in two halves, with hidden frame tubes, and a speedo that was set into a dash plate fitting between the two halves of the tank. The innovative design of the 1936 EL Knucklehead prevails in Harley-Davidsons today.

MILITARY MODELS

As the 30s continued, uncertainty and apprehension grew, with the possibility of war increasing in Europe, and the USA making preparations for intervention. Mechanization of the US Army's cavalry units began in the late 30s but it was not until 1940 that sufficient funds would be available to procure enough equipment to complete the process. Harley-Davidson sought to supply motorcycles to the army and shipped some WL models to Fort Knox for evaluation by the Mechanized Cavalry Board. Together with Indian, Harley-Davidson received small contracts to supply motorcycles. Harley's brief was to supply the WLA, an army version of their WL. The Canadian military also ordered a number of motorcycles, and a machine designated the WLC was built specifically for them, differing only slightly from the WLA.

The US Army's reorganization involved a new divisional structure. Each division was to consist of three independent Infantry Regiments and support units with sufficient transport to move regimental-sized groups. In addition, reconnaissance troops would ride at the front of each division, equipped with trucks and motorcycles. Of the latter, there were eight single bikes and three combinations per troop. Unlike the German army, who had machine-gun-toting sidecar outfits, the US army saw the motorcycle as a modern replacement for the horse, the idea being that the motorcycles would carry the scouts forward to where dismounted scouting could be carried out. This structure was quickly modified as other technology became available. The Jeep, which was introduced in 1941, was soon relegated to tasks away from the fighting. The bikes themselves became the workhorses of both despatch riders and military policemen and were in enough demand for Harley-Davidson to continue building military motorcycles for the duration of the war.

The WLA and WLCs changed slightly from year to year as refinements were made. Rubber parts, for example, were reduced on the bikes due to the short supply of the commodity after Japanese conquests of rubber-producing nations. Harley-Davidson made approximately 88,000 motorcycles during the war years and a large percentage of these were subsequently supplied to other allied nations. The factory received a number of accolades in the form of Army/Navy 'E for Excellence' awards for their efforts.

A PERIOD OF TRANSITION

Civilian production resumed after 1945, but things only really got back to normal in 1947, when raw materials became more freely available again. Boom years followed and in 1948 the company sold 31,163 bikes, but it was not to last. Imports from Europe flooded the US market and, in the face of stiff competition, Indian Motorcycles closed in 1953. Harley-Davidson preferred to compete head on and introduced a range of motorcycles designed to do exactly that.

The K Model was one such machine, a curious mixture of old and new components. The last 45 cu in (740 cc) W-series flathead was made in 1951, but a new flathead engine was fitted to the K Model. The K Model resembled its foreign competitors in styling in that it had a swinging-arm rear-suspension assembly, telescopic forks, foot-shift gear-change and neat compact lines. The side-valve engine was of unit construction but was vastly slower than the imports and as a result the KK Model was developed. A couple of years later, the KH Model was introduced, with a larger capacity that was capable of 95 mph (153 km/h). By the late 50s, side-valve engines were decidedly old-fashioned and in 1957 Harley-Davidson upgraded the motorcycle to accommodate overhead valves and redesignated it the XL. It was also known as the Sportster, a name still used on Harleys today.

The big twin-engined Harleys were also sequentially upgraded. The Panhead superseded the Knucklehead in 1948 but

For some fervent custom builders too much is never enough. This motorcycle in the Rat's Hole Custom Show in Daytona, Florida uses three Ironhead Sportster engines in a specially-made frame.

retained the E and F designations for the 61 cu in (1000 cc) and 74 cu in (1213 cc) models. The Panhead was essentially a new top end on the existing Knucklehead bottom end and, as the slang name implies, its rocker covers looked like upturned cooking pans. The cylinder heads were cast from aluminium after problems with the all-iron Knucklehead, hydraulic lifters contributed to a quieter running engine and a larger oil pump was used to improve lubrication. Improvements did not end there though. In 1949 the springer forks were replaced by hydraulic telescopic units on the Hydra Glide, the rigid frame was improved to swingarm rear suspension on the Duo Glide and the electric start that appeared in 1965 saw the big twin renamed the Electra Glide.

The Panhead engine gave way to the Shovelhead in 1966 and once again it was a new top on an existing bottom. The new engine became known as the Shovelhead because the rocker covers bore a resemblance to the backs of shovels. Most of the models had designations that started FL, with bikes such as the FLH, FLT, FLHB and so on. The Shovelhead was to take Harley through the 70s and the years of AMF ownership.

By the mid-60s Harley-Davidson's share of the US domestic motor-cycle market had contracted considerably, with a mere three per cent of its production being exported. Big twin Harleys from this era have surfaced in countries as far-flung and diverse as Vietnam, Iran and Nigeria. It soon became clear that Harley – the very last American motorcycle manufacturer – would go the way of Indian unless it received a substantial injection of dollars.

After negotiating with various potential buyers, Harley-Davidson was bought by American Machine and Foundry (AMF) on 7 January 1969. This huge conglomerate owned a variety of leisure and industrial companies. The takeover was not an entirely happy union – workers walked out over quality-control problems and job losses. Despite these difficulties, the early 70s were boom years for motorcycle sales and the AMF-controlled company was able to up production considerably. In the long term this strategy would compound the quality-control issue but such a consequence could not have been foreseen.

AMF are frequently criticized for their

The Harley-Davidson is the embodiment of America on two wheels, the motorcycling Red, White and Blue. The riders of this resplendent Heritage Softail proudly fly 'Old Glory' from the back of their machine.

style of ownership, but it is worth remembering that if AMF had not bought out Harley-Davidson in 1969, the company would not have survived.

MANAGEMENT BUY-OUT
In 1971, a new Harley-Davidson emerged – the FX Super Glide. This was an alternator Shovelhead with the slimmer Sportster front end. In many ways it was the first factory custom model and was also an attempt to compete with the unauthorized chopper-builders who thrived on chopping the dresser-style machines. There were a succession of FX models, each designating a particular detail such as electric start or disc brakes – the FXE, FXWG, FXDG, FXR, FXEF and FXB. Despite the popularity of the new model with long-time Harley enthusiasts, the 70s was the decade of a new generation of Japanese superbikes, and AMF began to reconsider its involvement in the Harley-Davidson operation.

In 1981, a group of 13 Harley-Davidson executives, led by Vaughan Beals, raised $100 million and bought the company from AMF. The advertising of the time was boosted by evocative lines such as 'The eagle soars alone . Easyriders magazine reported in April 1982 that 'Harley

currently sells only 31% of bikes in the over 1000 cc market. Honda has a 26% share, Kawasaki has 16% and the other Japanese manufacturers are coming on like Yamamoto at Pearl Harbor.' Vaughan Beals was interviewed on the reasons for AMF wanting to part with Harley-Davidson and was quoted as saying, 'Aggression is the key word in this industry. Without it you lose your market and AMF had lost the will to fight for Harley-Davidson's share of the market.' According to Beals, AMF had spent enormous sums on building and modernizing the Harley plants and had decided it was not willing to pump any more money into the firm. 'It had to justify Harley-Davidson's expenses against those of its 30 or 40 other businesses,' Beals recalled, 'But those of us who were running AMF's motorcycle products group had to justify what was right for Harley against what was right for AMF. It was a stand off.' He also added that, 'AMF considered our offer as a sort of last resort.'

HARLEY'S RESURGENCE
Though the eagle did soar alone, it immediately flew into difficult skies. Between 1980 and 1982, Harley-Davidson had to lay off a considerable number of its

Sturgis, South Dakota; in August one of two massive American biker gatherings is held here and bikers flock to it from far and wide. This is Sturgis Main Street: a similar gathering occurs every March at Daytona Beach, Florida.

workforce and the management appealed to the government to increase tariffs on imported Japanese motorcycles of over 43 cu in (700 cc) such as the Honda Goldwing. The Reagan administration imposed tariffs of up to 50 per cent on any Japanese imports and President Reagan himself went as far as visiting one of the Harley-Davidson plants.

Better days were ahead and in 1983 another new engine was announced. It was officially called the Evolution but soon gained the nickname of Blockhead, continuing the tradition of describing the rocker covers. It is now more generally referred to as the 'Evo'. The Evolution engine was to be Harley-Davidson's salvation and by 1984 its laid-off workers were re-employed, its market share had increased and the company had made a profit for the first time in three years. Vaughan Beals was quoted as saying that, 'We're not out of the woods yet but we're working hard to get there. We have an obligation to the American people and the government to take advantage of the breathing room the tariffs provide. We intend to fulfil that obligation by finishing up the job at hand.'

The first XL Sportster engine had displaced 54 cu in (883 cc), although by the early 70s there was a 61 cu in (1000 cc)

version available in a whole range of models such as the XL, XLCH, XLT and XLX. It remained in production until the introduction of the Evolution-engined Sportsters in 1986.

One Sportster different from others in the range was the XLCR of 1977. It was an XL Sportster with 'café racer' styling, hence the CR suffix to the designation. Although this was an attempt to put contemporary race styling onto the street, it was not particularly popular at the time. Now, however, such machines are highly sought-after. The XL Sportster formed the basis of Harley-Davidson's competition bikes; dirt- and flat-track racing are popular forms of competitive motorcycling in the USA. As a result, competition-inspired models such as the XR1000 featured in Harley's 1983 model range.

The Sportster received a redesign in 1978 when it was given a new frame although the engine did not change until 1986, when the Evolution-engined Sportster appeared as a 54 cu in (883 cc) machine. The range was then extended with the addition of a 67 cu in (1100 cc) model, later increased to 74 cu in (1200 cc). The new engine components were particularly noted for reducing excessive wear and oil consumption. Transmission was upgraded from four- to five-speed to take advantage

of the improved engine and keep up with the worldwide trend towards five- and six-speed motorcycles.

SUCCESSFUL EVOLUTION

The Evolution engine is the one factor above all else that saved Harley-Davidson from going out of business and turned them into a major force. It was in many ways a much improved Shovelhead engine, using alloy cylinder barrels and heads which permit greater and more even heat dissipation than the iron and alloy combination of the Shovelhead. Also improved were levels of quality control, oil consumption and frequency of maintenance. The entire range of big-twins benefited from the new engine and the range was extended in 1984 with the introduction of a new model, the Softail.

The Softail models were based around a specific new type of frame. It had the appearance of a vintage rigid frame but featured suspension. The nostalgic look received another boost with the introduction of the Softail Springer and the Softail Custom. The Springer came with what had previously been considered completely outmoded 'springer' forks, while the Custom appeared to have after-market parts and paint schemes.

Alongside the Softail range came the FXR range – the R suffix signified a rubber-mounted engine and a redesigned frame. It was followed in 1991 by the Dyna Glide and the FXDB Sturgis (named after one of America's biggest biker gatherings). Since then there have been other models, such as the Bad Boy, which was almost as close as a major factory could come to building a chopper. All are based around the Evolution engine – a name that is entirely appropriate as the bottom end of the 80 cu in (1340 cc) engine can trace its origins back through the Shovelhead and Panhead to the original 61E Knucklehead of 1936.

This could be the final chapter in Harley-Davidson's history of producing air-cooled engines, as increasingly stringent emissions regulations could mean that liquid-cooled engines will power Harleys of the future. In recent years Harley-Davidson have actually been promoting a liquid-cooled race bike – the VR1000. It has not been without its problems, but then again, what developmental machine isn't?

1942 WLA

A military version of the WL, the WLA was introduced at a time when the US army saw the potential for motorcycles to be used in a battlefield situation. The WLA was heavier but stronger than the WL, and over 88,000 of them were produced for military use, seeing action all over the world.

Both military and civilian WL models featured hand-shift transmission – the gear lever had to be moved forwards from neutral into first and then backwards for second and third.

In early models, the dash panel in the tank was referred to as the 'cat's eye dash' because of the shape of the warning light lenses. Gas went in the left filler cap and oil in the right.

Harley-Davidson's post-war tail-light, introduced in 1947, was referred to as the 'tombstone' tail-light because of the resemblance of the shape of the lens to an old-style tombstone.

SPECIFICATION

1942 WLC Civilianized

Owner:	Leo Keizer
	Delft, Holland

ENGINE

Model:	Flathead
Capacity:	45 cu in (740 cc)
Cases:	HD
Carb:	Linkert
Air filter:	pancake
Ignition:	points
Pipes:	standard fishtail muffler

TRANSMISSION

Type:	three speed

FRAME

Model:	rigid WL

SUSPENSION

Front:	springer forks
Rear:	none

WHEELS AND BRAKES

Front:	16 in (41 cm) spoked
Brake:	drum
Rear:	16 in (41 cm) spoked
Brake:	drum

FENDERS

Front:	civilian WL
Rear:	civilian WL

ACCESSORIES

Handlebars:	Buckhorn
Risers:	none
Headlight:	WL
Tail-light:	HD Tombstone
Clocks:	dash mounted
Tank:	3.5-gallon (13.2-litre) Fatbob
Oil tank:	integral with fuel tank
Seat:	HD Buddy seat
Footrests:	footboards
Electrics:	six-volt

PAINT AND FINISH

Paint:	civilian
Colour:	black/white
Chrome/polish:	chromed accessories

1942 WLC Civilianized

In the USA, surplus army bikes were put up for sale, while in countries such as Holland, Harleys left by the Allied Forces were sold on. This particular machine is a WLC that was sold in Holland.

Many owners repainted their old army machines and fitted chromed parts. The military fittings from this bike have gone and have been replaced with their civilian equivalents, including the air filter, tail-light, saddle, handlebars, fenders, kick starter and gear change.

1942 WLA

As the world drifted towards war, the United States began to modernize its army.

Progressive military staff realised that the nature of warfare was changing and that mobility would be the key to success in future battlefield confrontations.

The US Army acquired motorcycles because they saw how important a role they could play in delivering messages between the diverse parts of an army as well as their potential as scouting and reconnaissance vehicles.

Harley-Davidson received orders for large numbers of the WLA model. The suffix A indicated that it was an army version of the WL.

It differed from the WL in a number of ways – gloss paint and chrome plate were eliminated and the fenders were redesigned, a strong rear rack was fixed over the rear fender, and twin military tail-lights and smaller blackout lamp were fitted.

The leather rifle holster was carried in a specially designed bracket that fitted on the side of the front forks and had an ammunition box on the other side.

lianized

1942 WLC Civi

War-surplus Harley-Davidsons were purchased by transport-hungry civilians and many were converted to a civilian specification by enthusiastic owners. The WLC was the Canadian version of the military WL.

The heavy-duty rear rack fitted to the WLA could carry both the traditional saddlebags and also a standard military radio. Twin tail-lights were standard on all US Army vehicles.

The rifle rack and ammunition box were fitted to US Army WLAs intended for use in combat areas; the standard vehicle blackout lamp was fitted to WLAs used in all areas of operation.

The speedo was mounted in a dash in the tanks as on the civilian models, while the brass plaque immediately in front of the saddle provided lubrication information for the rider.

SPECIFICATION

1942 WLA

Owner:	Peter Buchly
	Rijswijk, Holland

ENGINE

Model:	Flathead
Capacity:	45 cu in (740 cc)
Cases:	HD
Carb:	Linkert
Air filter:	oil bath
Ignition:	points
Pipes:	flat black muffler

TRANSMISSION

Type:	three speed

FRAME

Model:	rigid military version of WL

SUSPENSION

Front:	springer forks
Rear:	none

WHEELS AND BRAKES

Front:	18 in (46 cm)
Brake:	drum
Rear:	18 in (46 cm)
Brake:	drum

FENDERS

Front:	military specification
Rear:	military specification

ACCESSORIES

Handlebars:	military specification
Risers:	none
Headlight:	military specification
Tail-light:	twin military
Clocks:	tank-mounted speedo
Tank:	3.5-gallon (13.2-litre) Fatbob
Oil tank:	integral with fuel tank
Seat:	sprung saddle
Footrests:	footboards
Electrics:	six-volt

PAINT AND FINISH

Paint:	military specification
Colour:	olive drab
Chrome/polish:	none

Both military and civilian WL models featured hand-shift transmission – the gear lever had to be moved forwards from neutral into first and then backwards for second and third.

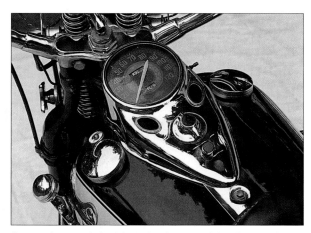

In early models, the dash panel in the tank was referred to as the 'cat's eye dash' because of the shape of the warning light lenses. Gas went in the left filler cap and oil in the right.

Harley-Davidson's post-war tail-light, introduced in 1947, was referred to as the 'tombstone' tail-light because of the resemblance of the shape of the lens to an old-style tombstone.

SPECIFICATION

1942 WLC Civilianized

Owner:	Leo Keizer
	Delft, Holland

ENGINE

Model:	Flathead
Capacity:	45 cu in (740 cc)
Cases:	HD
Carb:	Linkert
Air filter:	pancake
Ignition:	points
Pipes:	standard fishtail muffler

TRANSMISSION

Type:	three speed

FRAME

Model:	rigid WL

SUSPENSION

Front:	springer forks
Rear:	none

WHEELS AND BRAKES

Front:	16 in (41 cm) spoked
Brake:	drum
Rear:	16 in (41 cm) spoked
Brake:	drum

FENDERS

Front:	civilian WL
Rear:	civilian WL

ACCESSORIES

Handlebars:	Buckhorn
Risers:	none
Headlight:	WL
Tail-light:	HD Tombstone
Clocks:	dash mounted
Tank:	3.5-gallon (13.2-litre) Fatbob
Oil tank:	integral with fuel tank
Seat:	HD Buddy seat
Footrests:	footboards
Electrics:	six-volt

PAINT AND FINISH

Paint:	civilian
Colour:	black/white
Chrome/polish:	chromed accessories

1942 WLA

A military version of the WL, the WLA was introduced at a time when the US army saw the potential for motorcycles to be used in a battlefield situation. The WLA was heavier but stronger than the WL, and over 88,000 of them were produced for military use, seeing action all over the world.

The heavy-duty rear rack fitted to the WLA could carry both the traditional saddlebags and also a standard military radio. Twin tail-lights were standard on all US Army vehicles.

The rifle rack and ammunition box were fitted to US Army WLAs intended for use in combat areas; the standard vehicle blackout lamp was fitted to WLAs used in all areas of operation.

The speedo was mounted in a dash in the tanks as on the civilian models, while the brass plaque immediately in front of the saddle provided lubrication information for the rider.

SPECIFICATION

1942 WLA

Owner:	Peter Buchly
	Rijswijk, Holland

ENGINE

Model:	Flathead
Capacity:	45 cu in (740 cc)
Cases:	HD
Carb:	Linkert
Air filter:	oil bath
Ignition:	points
Pipes:	flat black muffler

TRANSMISSION

Type:	three speed

FRAME

Model:	rigid military version of WL

SUSPENSION

Front:	springer forks
Rear:	none

WHEELS AND BRAKES

Front:	18 in (46 cm)
Brake:	drum
Rear:	18 in (46 cm)
Brake:	drum

FENDERS

Front:	military specification
Rear:	military specification

ACCESSORIES

Handlebars:	military specification
Risers:	none
Headlight:	military specification
Tail-light:	twin military
Clocks:	tank-mounted speedo
Tank:	3.5-gallon (13.2-litre) Fatbob
Oil tank:	integral with fuel tank
Seat:	sprung saddle
Footrests:	footboards
Electrics:	six-volt

PAINT AND FINISH

Paint:	military specification
Colour:	olive drab
Chrome/polish:	none

1942 WLC Civi

War-surplus Harley-Davidsons were purchased by transport-hungry civilians and many were converted to a civilian specification by enthusiastic owners. The WLC was the Canadian version of the military WL.

lianized

1942 WLA

As the world drifted towards war, the United States began to modernize its army.

Progressive military staff realised that the nature of warfare was changing and that mobility would be the key to success in future battlefield confrontations.

The US Army acquired motorcycles because they saw how important a role they could play in delivering messages between the diverse parts of an army as well as their potential as scouting and reconnaissance vehicles.

Harley-Davidson received orders for large numbers of the WLA model. The suffix A indicated that it was an army version of the WL.

It differed from the WL in a number of ways – gloss paint and chrome plate were eliminated and the fenders were redesigned, a strong rear rack was fixed over the rear fender, and twin military tail-lights and smaller blackout lamp were fitted.

The leather rifle holster was carried in a specially designed bracket that fitted on the side of the front forks and had an ammunition box on the other side.

1942 WLC Civilianized

In the USA, surplus army bikes were put up for sale, while in countries such as Holland, Harleys left by the Allied Forces were sold on. This particular machine is a WLC that was sold in Holland.

Many owners repainted their old army machines and fitted chromed parts. The military fittings from this bike have gone and have been replaced with their civilian equivalents, including the air filter, tail-light, saddle, handlebars, fenders, kick starter and gear change.

Knucklehead

At the end of World War II Harley-Davidson resumed civilian production, initially reintroducing motorcycles from its pre-war range. The 1947 Knucklehead was one of those machines. It is generally accepted that the 61E is the model from which all current Harleys draw their styling.

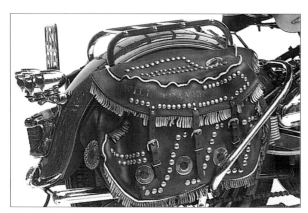

Harley-Davidson have always produced bike accessories. In the late 40s items such as these saddlebags were listed in the official Harley catalogues.

While the WL models stayed essentially the same for many years, the tank badges, chrome trims and colour schemes varied each year. The spotlights were an accessory.

Although the 45 cu in (740 cc) side-valve engine would only remain in the WL for a few years after 1947, it was used until the early 70s to power the three-wheeled Servicar.

SPECIFICATION

1947 WL

Owner:	Lou Marlow
	London, England

ENGINE

Model:	WL side-valve
Capacity:	45 cu in (740 cc)
Cases:	HD
Carb:	Linkert
Air filter:	circular with mesh element
Ignition:	points
Pipes:	fishtail muffler

TRANSMISSION

Type:	three speed

FRAME

Model:	rigid WL

SUSPENSION

Front:	springer forks
Rear:	none

WHEELS AND BRAKES

Front:	16 in (41 cm)
Brake:	drum
Rear:	16 in (41 cm)
Brake:	drum

FENDERS

Front:	steel WL
Rear:	steel WL

ACCESSORIES

Handlebars:	HD WL
Risers:	none
Headlight:	chromed 6 in (15 cm)
Tail-light:	HD beehive
Clocks:	tank-mounted speedo
Tank:	3.5-gallon (13.2-litre) Fatbob
Oil tank:	integral with fuel tank
Seat:	sprung solo saddle
Footrests:	footboards
Electrics:	six-volt

PAINT AND FINISH

Paint:	two-tone
Colour:	red/grey
Chrome/polish:	numerous chrome accessories

1947 61E Knucklehead

The Knucklehead was available as a 61 cu in (1000 cc) machine from 1936 (the 61E) and as a 74 cu in (1200 cc) from 1941 (the 61F). Production of both models was suspended in 1941 after the Japanese air strike against Pearl Harbor, but resumed briefly after the war. It was superseded by the Panhead, albeit with a similar frame and cycle parts.

1947 WL

The first of the 45 cu in (740 cc) side-valve engines were unveiled in 1928. In 1937 they were named the W Series. Although not as fast as the Indian Sport Scout with which it was in competition, the W Series was sturdier and more reliable. These 45s formed the basis of Harley's success.

The new post-war tank-mounted dash panel is generally referred to as the 'two-light dash' to differentiate it from the earlier cat's eye dash and the later three-light version.

The front-fender running light and the chrome fender-edge trim are typical of the era when this Knucklehead was built. A fender lamp was a stock item, but the trim was an accessory.

The Knucklehead was replaced in 1948 by the Panhead, with essentially new barrels and heads on the Knucklehead crank cases. It retained the ribbed timing cover seen here.

SPECIFICATION

1947 61E Knucklehead

| Owner: | Stuart Hall |
| | Manchester, England |

ENGINE

Model:	Knucklehead
Capacity:	61 cu in (1000 cc)
Cases:	HD
Carb:	Linkert
Air filter:	circular pancake
Ignition:	points
Pipes:	two-into-one muffler

TRANSMISSION

Type:	four speed

FRAME

Model:	rigid EL

SUSPENSION

Front:	springer forks
Rear:	none

WHEELS AND BRAKES

Front:	16 in (41 cm) spoked
Brake:	drum
Rear:	16 in (41 cm) spoked
Brake:	drum

FENDERS

Front:	HD EL
Rear:	HD EL

ACCESSORIES

Handlebars:	HD stock
Risers:	none
Headlight:	chromed 6 in (15 cm)
Tail-light:	tombstone
Clocks:	tank-mounted dash panel
Tank:	Fatbob
Oil tank:	horseshoe
Seat:	solo saddle
Footrests:	footboards
Electrics:	six-volt

PAINT AND FINISH

Paint:	gloss black
Colour:	black
Chrome/polish:	HD chrome parts

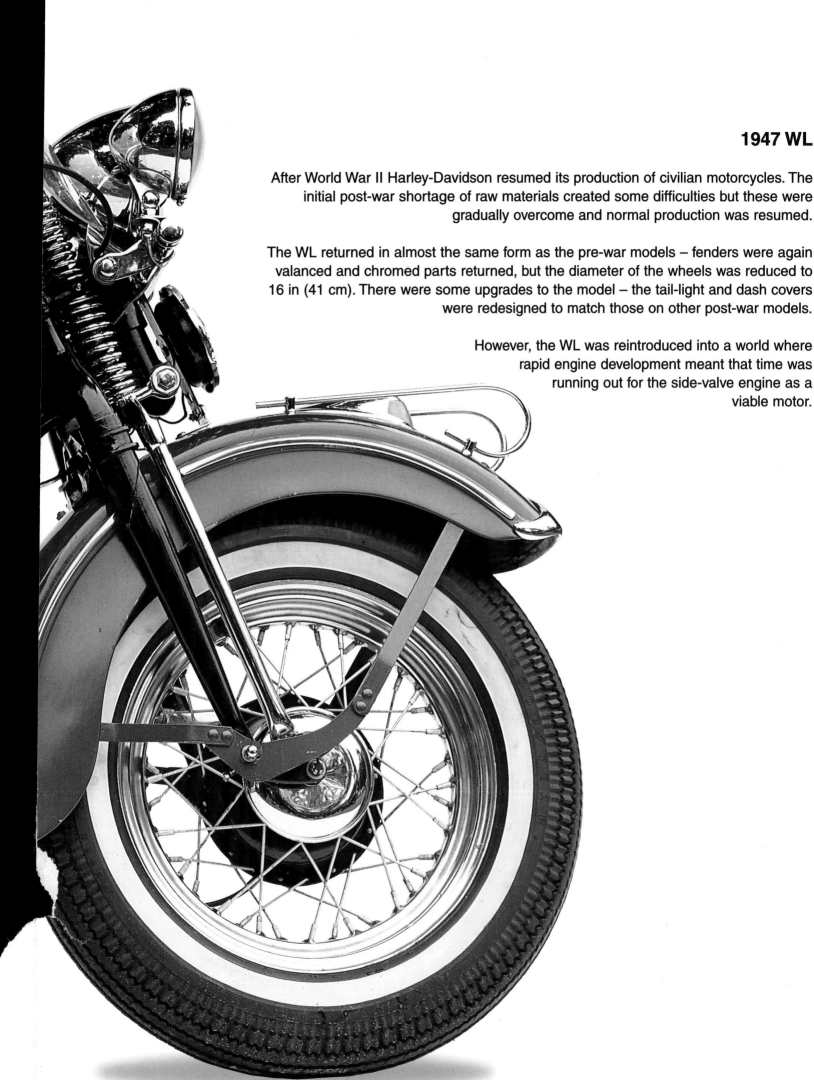

1947 WL

After World War II Harley-Davidson resumed its production of civilian motorcycles. The initial post-war shortage of raw materials created some difficulties but these were gradually overcome and normal production was resumed.

The WL returned in almost the same form as the pre-war models – fenders were again valanced and chromed parts returned, but the diameter of the wheels was reduced to 16 in (41 cm). There were some upgrades to the model – the tail-light and dash covers were redesigned to match those on other post-war models.

However, the WL was reintroduced into a world where rapid engine development meant that time was running out for the side-valve engine as a viable motor.

Harley-Davidson were proud that they had produced a Big Twin with rear suspension to complement the smaller K series, and displayed the badge on the FL front fender.

The rear suspension components meant that the teardrop-shaped toolbox – a feature of Harleys since before World War II – had to be repositioned vertically.

This particular model is an FL because it still features a hand-shift and therefore foot-clutch gearchange. The FLF with hand-clutch and foot-shift had been available since 1952.

SPECIFICATION

1958 FL Duo Glide

Owner:	Terry Sweeney Swindon, England

ENGINE

Model:	Panhead
Capacity:	74 cu in (1200 cc)
Cases:	HD
Carb:	stock HD
Air filter:	circular chrome
Ignition:	points
Pipes:	two-into-one

TRANSMISSION

Type:	four speed

FRAME

Model:	swingarm FL Duoglide

SUSPENSION

Front:	telescopic forks
Rear:	swingarm and shock absorbers

WHEELS AND BRAKES

Front:	16 in (41 cm) spoked
Brake:	drum
Rear:	16 in (41 cm) spoked
Brake:	drum

FENDERS

Front:	FL
Rear:	FL

ACCESSORIES

Handlebars:	dresser
Risers:	none
Headlight:	9 in (23 cm)
Tail-light:	stock HD
Clocks:	tank-mounted dash
Tank:	Fatbob
Oil tank:	chromed horseshoe
Seat:	solo saddle
Footrests:	footboards
Electrics:	six-volt

PAINT AND FINISH

Paint:	HD
Colour:	two-tone black/white
Chrome/polish:	stock HD

FL Hydra Glide

The Hydra Glide was the first Harley-Davidson to feature hydraulic telescopic forks. It was powered by the Panhead engine, which had been introduced into the springer-forked frame a year prior to the introduction of the hydraulic forks in 1949.

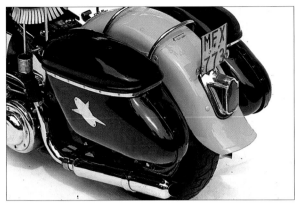

The saddlebags were period accessories and followed the curves of the rear fender, which is hinged to enable the rear wheel to be changed and the chain to be adjusted.

The decorated saddle, which features fringes and conchos, is designed for two people and has handles fitted for the convenience and safety of the pillion passenger.

This Hydra Glide has exhaust pipes that run either side of the rear wheel. The chromed, teardrop-shaped item is a locking toolbox bolted to brackets welded to the rigid frame.

SPECIFICATION

1953 FL Hydra Glide

Owner:	Michel Nivarlet
	Liege, Belgium

ENGINE

Model:	Panhead
Capacity:	74 cu in (1200 cc)
Cases:	HD
Carb:	Linkert
Air filter:	circular chrome
Ignition:	points
Pipes:	HD muffler

TRANSMISSION

Type:	four speed

FRAME

Model:	rigid Hydra Glide

SUSPENSION

Front:	telescopic forks
Rear:	none

WHEELS AND BRAKES

Front:	16 in (41 cm) spoked
Brake:	drum
Rear:	16 in (41 cm) spoked
Brake:	drum

FENDERS

Front:	HD FL
Rear:	HD FL

ACCESSORIES

Handlebars:	dresser
Risers:	none
Headlight:	9 in (23 cm)
Tail-light:	tombstone
Clocks:	dash-mounted speedo
Tank:	Fatbob
Oil tank:	chromed horseshoe
Seat:	buddy seat
Footrests:	footboards
Electrics:	12-volt

PAINT AND FINISH

Paint:	HD
Colour:	blue
Chrome/polish:	HD stock and accessories

FL Duo Glide

The Duo Glide was the logical extension of the Hydra Glide – a big twin with two suspension systems (glides), hence its name. It was introduced in 1958, by which time Harley-Davidson was the last remaining US motorcycle manufacturer.

1953 FL Hydra Glide

The Hydra Glide was introduced in 1949 and replaced the springer-forked Panhead. It remained in production until superseded by the Duo Glide in 1958.

This motorcycle was made in 1953 and was powered by the Panhead engine in its 74 cu in (1200 cc) displacement form.

The Hydra Glide did not feature rear suspension but relied on the sprung saddle to ensure the rider's comfort.

The elongated saddle on this machine is known as a 'buddy seat' as it was intended to seat two people; the handles on the rear corners were for the pillion passenger to hold on to.

The panniers and windshield helped make the Hydra Glide suitable for long distance journeys.

1958 FL Duo Glide

The Duo Glide retained the FL designation of the Hydra Glide while a more powerful FLH model was also available.

The bike's get up and go was supplied by the Panhead engine, and there were a number of variants. The original Panhead was upgraded in 1955 and the earlier E and F models, with lower compression, were dropped. The updated variant, with a new bottom end incorporating stronger bearings, was suitable for the FLH model.

The Duo Glide was available with both hand- and foot-shift gear changes. The FLF was the foot-shift hand-clutch variant.

The styling of this Duo Glide is typical of its time; chrome trims, whitewall tyres and two-tone paint – features evident on both motorcycles and cars of the late 50s.

1956 KH900 Sportster

The KH was a developed version of the K model which itself was in some ways an updated WL model.

The K model was a unit construction side-valve V-twin, built with foot-change hand clutch transmission and aimed at competing with the British bikes imported from Europe in the years after World War II.

The main drawback with the K model was that its performance did not match those of the imports, so in 1954 the KH was introduced.

It was a K model engine with a lengthened stroke, which meant its displacement was increased to 54 cu in (883 cc).

It also had new flywheels, cylinder barrels and an improved clutch and was an overall better machine, one that could compete with the British imports on more even terms.

It remained in production until 1956 when it was replaced by the XL models, the first of the Harley motorcycles referred to as Sportsters.

1961 Duo Glide

The suspension system at the front end of the Duo Glide remained as before, with hydraulic telescopic forks, while the rear was upgraded through the introduction of a swingarm and a pair of shock absorbers.

The Duo Glide was available with hand-shift gear change (the FL) and foot-shift gear change (the FLF). Harley-Davidson kept both models in production alongside one another as the FL was still in demand from their more traditional customers. This 1961 model features a foot-clutch and hand-shift gear box.

KH900 Sportster

The K Series was introduced to compete with successful British twins produced in the years after World War II. The KH Sportster had a bored-out version of the side-valve 45 engine but was nevertheless regarded as a sluggish machine.

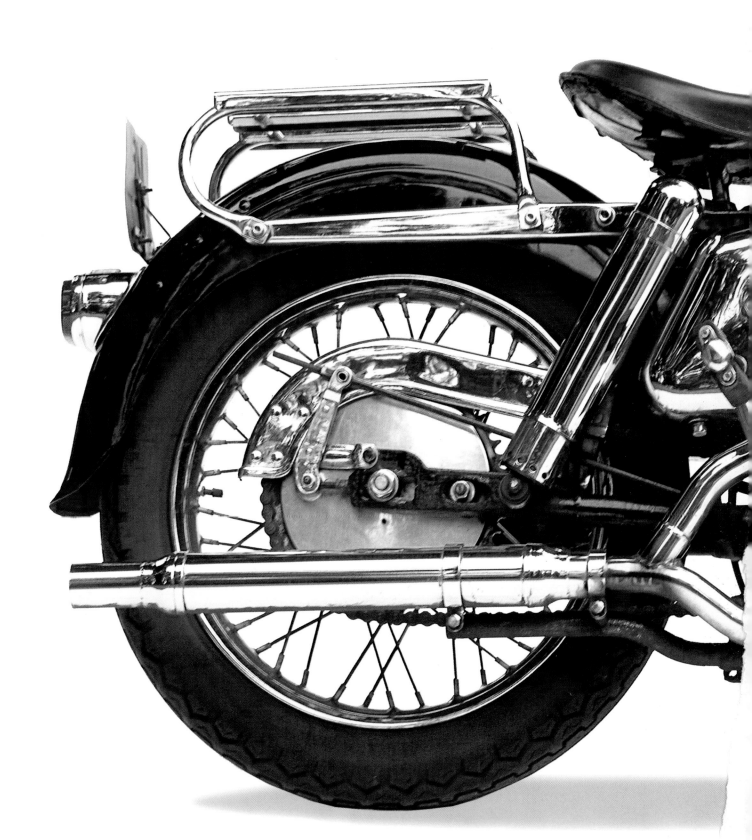

This bike's new feature was the rear suspension. The swingarm is visible below the studded saddlebag while the chromed shock absorber is seen in front of it.

The name Duo Glide indicates that the FL had both front and rear suspension. Harley-Davidson fitted this chromed badge either side of the front fender to show this feature.

50s and 60s FL models feature this cast alloy headlamp nacelle into which a large headlamp was fitted. The tank badges varied from year to year, as did the paint schemes.

SPECIFICATION

1961 Duo Glide

Owner:	Martin Snippert
	Bakkerskamp, Holland

ENGINE

Model:	Panhead
Capacity:	74 cu in (1200 cc)
Cases:	HD
Carb:	Linkert
Air filter:	pancake
Ignition:	points
Pipes:	fishtail muffler

TRANSMISSION

Type:	four speed

FRAME

Model:	swingarm Duo Glide

SUSPENSION

Front:	telescopic forks
Rear:	swingarm and shock absorbers

WHEELS AND BRAKES

Front:	16 in (41 cm) spoked
Brake:	drum
Rear:	16 in (41 cm) spoked
Brake:	drum

FENDERS

Front:	HD FL
Rear:	HD FL

ACCESSORIES

Handlebars:	dresser
Risers:	none
Headlight:	cast nacelle
Tail-light:	HD stock
Clocks:	dash-mounted speedo
Tank:	Fatbob
Oil tank:	horseshoe
Seat:	solo saddle
Footrests:	footboards
Electrics:	12-volt

PAINT AND FINISH

Paint:	two-tone
Colour:	black/white
Chrome/polish:	stock HD chrome and aluminium

Duo Glide

The Duo Glide was a refined version of the Hydra Glide, and retained its FL designation. It was updated by the addition of a second suspension system at the rear.

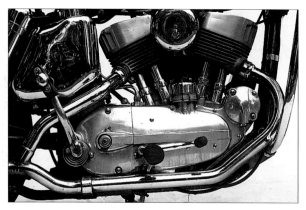

The side-valve KH engine was the first of the unit-construction Harley-Davidson engines to displace 54 cu in (883 cc). This displacement is still found in Sportsters today.

The smaller gas tank precluded the mounting of the speedo in the tank-dash. Later Sportsters had the speedo mounted on a bracket from the handlebar clamp.

The KH model was intended to compete with imported British bikes and had some similar features. This drum brake is very British in appearance and laced to a 19 in (48 cm) rim.

SPECIFICATION

1956 KH900 Sportster

Owner:	Anon

ENGINE

Model:	KH
Capacity:	54 cu in (883 cc)
Cases:	HD
Carb:	Linkert
Air filter:	circular chrome
Ignition:	points
Pipes:	two-into-one

TRANSMISSION

Type:	four speed

FRAME

Model:	swingarm KH

SUSPENSION

Front:	telescopic forks
Rear:	swingarm and shock absorbers

WHEELS AND BRAKES

Front:	19 in (48 cm) spoked
Brake:	drum
Rear:	18 in (46 cm) spoked
Brake:	drum

FENDERS

Front:	KH
Rear:	KH

ACCESSORIES

Handlebars:	buckhorn
Risers:	none
Headlight:	9 in (23 cm)
Tail-light:	stock HD
Clocks:	mounted in fork shroud
Tank:	KH
Oil tank:	under seat
Seat:	solo saddle
Footrests:	footpegs
Electrics:	six-volt

PAINT AND FINISH

Paint:	HD
Colour:	black
Chrome/polish:	stock HD

1976 FLH Shovelhead

The style of motorcycle constructed by Harley-Davidson, their method of construction and the fact that many parts are interchangeable has encouraged a growth in after-market parts manufacture. This has encouraged riders to customize their bikes to suit their own tastes and riding styles.

This Shovelhead has been tastefully modified with extra chrome parts as well as different turn signals and tank badges. The turn signals are from a later bike and the tank badges from a 1965 model. The black and white two-tone paint finish is flawless.

The saddlebags, handlebar, clutch and brake controls, exhaust pipes, carburettor and air filter are all custom parts.

The bike has an alternator Shovelhead engine – the DC generator was replaced by an AC alternator in 1970.

ide

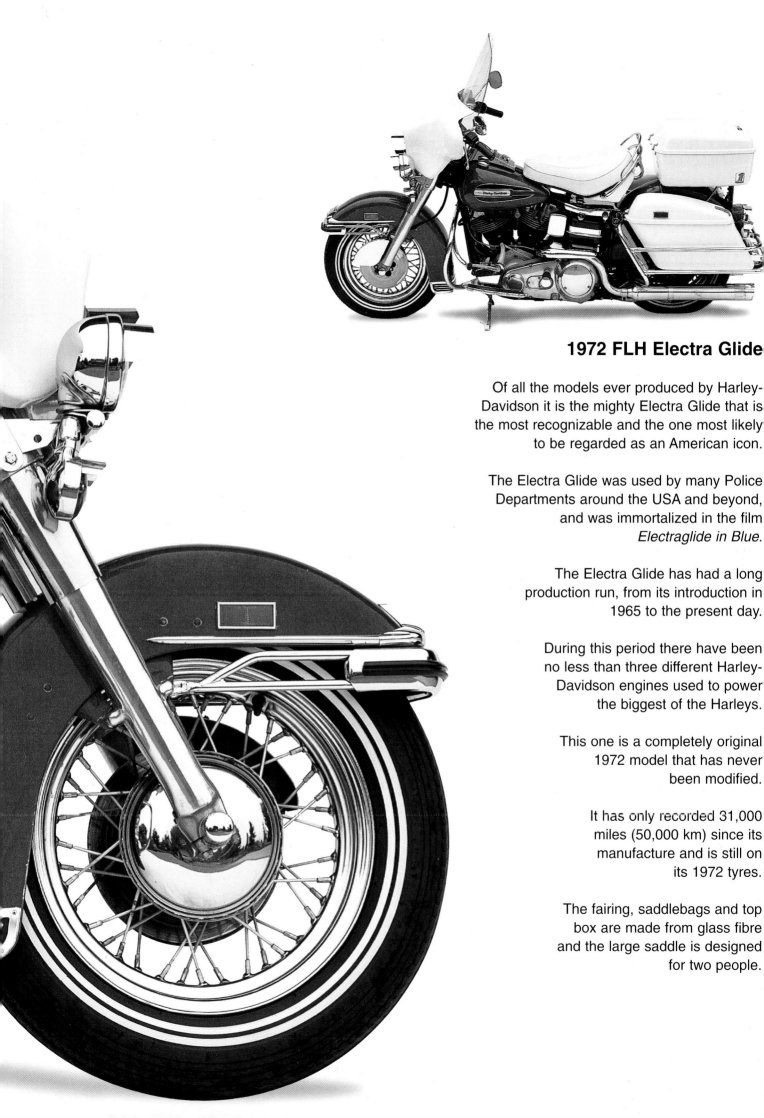

1972 FLH Electra Glide

Of all the models ever produced by Harley-Davidson it is the mighty Electra Glide that is the most recognizable and the one most likely to be regarded as an American icon.

The Electra Glide was used by many Police Departments around the USA and beyond, and was immortalized in the film *Electraglide in Blue*.

The Electra Glide has had a long production run, from its introduction in 1965 to the present day.

During this period there have been no less than three different Harley-Davidson engines used to power the biggest of the Harleys.

This one is a completely original 1972 model that has never been modified.

It has only recorded 31,000 miles (50,000 km) since its manufacture and is still on its 1972 tyres.

The fairing, saddlebags and top box are made from glass fibre and the large saddle is designed for two people.

FLH Shovelhead

This 1976 FLH dates from the year of America's bicentennial. It is typical of many Harleys in that it has been slightly modified by its owner although it still has the unmistakable look of a standard Harley-Davidson.

This motorcycle has changed so little that it is still fitted with its original Goodyear dual whitewall tyres. The chromed disc brake cover was an accessory typical of the 70s.

During AMF's ownership of Harley-Davidson a popular trademark was the stars and stripes logo, seen here on the points cover of the alternator-Shovelhead's engine.

The 12-volt battery is carried beneath the upper frame tube and concealed behind this square chrome cover. The oil tank is in the corresponding position on the other side.

SPECIFICATION

1972 FLH Electra Glide

| Owner: | Dale Richardson |
| | Greeley, Colorado |

ENGINE

Model:	Shovelhead
Capacity:	74 cu in (1200 cc)
Cases:	HD
Carb:	stock HD
Air filter:	HD oval
Ignition:	points
Pipes:	stock muffler

TRANSMISSION

Type:	four speed

FRAME

Model:	swingarm FLH

SUSPENSION

Front:	telescopic forks
Rear:	swingarm and shock absorbers

WHEELS AND BRAKES

Front:	16 in (41 cm) spoked
Brake:	single disc
Rear:	16 in (41 cm) spoked
Brake:	drum

FENDERS

Front:	stock FLH
Rear:	stock FLH

ACCESSORIES

Handlebars:	dresser
Risers:	none
Headlight:	9 in (23 cm)
Tail-light:	HD stock with spotlights
Clocks:	tank-mounted dash panel
Tank:	Fatbob
Oil tank:	square under seat
Seat:	buddy seat
Footrests:	footboards and footpegs
Electrics:	12-volt

PAINT AND FINISH

Paint:	HD
Colour:	hi-fi red
Chrome/polish:	HD chrome and alloy parts

FLH Electra G

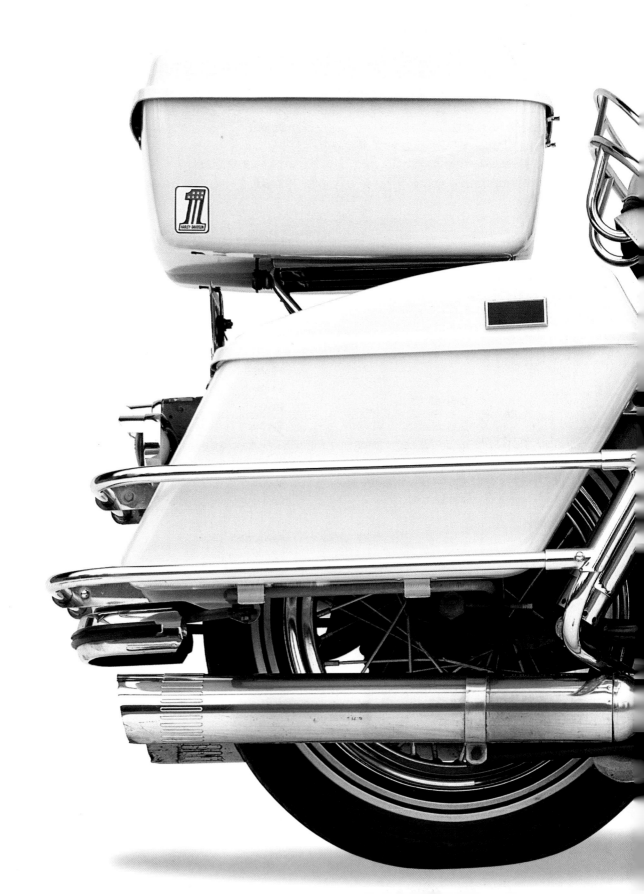

The brake caliper used on 70s' AMF-era Harleys such as this was also used on aircraft. While modern calipers are more compact, the design of disc rotor has changed little.

The lines of the Fatbob tank and the dash mounted within it are timeless Harley-Davidson – these tank badges date from 1965 and the dash is mid-70s.

The rear brake is partially concealed behind the saddlebags. The hub accepts the brake disc on one side and the drive sprocket on the other and is known as a dual flange hub.

SPECIFICATION

1976 FLH Shovelhead

Owner:	Dale Richardson
	Greeley, Colorado

ENGINE

Model:	Shovelhead
Capacity:	74 cu in (1200 cc)
Cases:	HD
Carb:	Screamin' Eagle
Air filter:	Screamin' Eagle
Ignition:	points
Pipes:	slash cut

TRANSMISSION

Type:	four speed

FRAME

Model:	swingarm FLH

SUSPENSION

Front:	telescopic forks
Rear:	swingarm and shock absorbers

WHEELS AND BRAKES

Front:	16 in (41 cm) spoked
Brake:	single disc
Rear:	16 in (41 cm) spoked
Brake:	disc

FENDERS

Front:	stock FLH
Rear:	stock FLH

ACCESSORIES

Handlebars:	dresser bars
Risers:	none
Headlight:	Nacelle mounted 9 in (23 cm)
Tail-light:	HD with blue dot
Clocks:	tank-mounted dash panel
Tank:	Fatbob
Oil tank:	square
Seat:	solo saddle
Footrests:	footboards
Electrics:	12-volt

PAINT AND FINISH

Paint:	two-tone
Colour:	black/white
Chrome/polish:	HD and some accessories

1983 XR1000

The XR1000 engine used an XL1000 bottom end with cylinder heads, exhausts and carburettors from the XR750 racing engine.

The barrels were new components. The dual carburettors were positioned on the right side of the engine and the exhaust pipes on the left. The remainder of the machine was almost all the stock XLX Sportster.

Because the XR1000 was a limited edition model and made from an unusual combination of parts, it retailed for a higher price than the other Sportsters in the early 80s range.

Despite this it was a fast motorcycle and the first Harley that achieved drag-strip quarter-mile (400-m) times of less than 13 seconds.

1978 XLCR Café Race[r]

In late 1977 Harley-Davidson introduced [a]
radically restyled Sportster that feature[d]
European café racer styling – racetrack look[s]
for everyday street use[.]

The CR suffix to the XL Sportster designatio[n]
stood for Café Racer and was prominent[ly]
displayed on the primary cove[r]

With the exception of the Siamese[d]
exhaust pipes, which were matt black, th[e]
new Sportster was a striking gloss blac[k]
all ove[r]

The remainder of the bike wa[s]
finished in chrome and polishe[d]
alloy. Items such as the gas tan[k]
had been redesigned and the se[at]
was clearly race-track inspire[d]

The rear portion of the frame wa[s]
based on the styling of the XR75[0]
but the whole unit was stretche[d]
to allow the oil tank and batte[ry]
to be fitted; as a result, th[e]
shock absorbers were mounte[d]
further back than on other mode[ls]

Rear set brake and gear-chang[e]
mechanisms allowed the rider [to]
assume a sports-bike riding positio[n]
Cast alloy Morris wheels and Kels[ey]
Hayes disc brakes completed t[he]
sporty appearanc[e]

XR1000

The XR1000 was a competition-inspired bike manufactured and marketed for the street. In many ways it was a styling exercise, as the bike was a mixture of Sportster XL1000 street parts and XR750 race parts.

The XLCR featured a race-style seat and tailpiece that was manufactured especially for the model. The frame was lengthened to allow the repositioning of the shock absorbers.

The majority of the XLCR was finished in black, including the engine and primary cover in wrinkle finish, while much of the remainder was sprayed gloss black.

The glass fibre bikini fairing and elongated gas tank were made especially for the XLCR and no doubt enhance the café racer appeal of the machine.

SPECIFICATION

1978 XLCR Café Racer

Owner:	Vince Martin
	Southampton, England

ENGINE

Model:	Sportster
Capacity:	61 cu in (1000 cc)
Cases:	HD
Carb:	stock HD
Air filter:	black race-track oval
Ignition:	points
Pipes:	Siamesed two-into-one

TRANSMISSION

Type:	four speed

FRAME

Model:	swingarm XLCR

SUSPENSION

Front:	telescopic forks
Rear:	swingarm

WHEELS AND BRAKES

Front:	19 in (48 cm) cast seven spoke
Brake:	twin disc
Rear:	18 in (46 cm) cast seven spoke
Brake:	disc

FENDERS

Front:	XLCR
Rear:	race-style

ACCESSORIES

Handlebars:	flat
Risers:	none
Headlight:	in fairing
Tail-light:	stock HD
Clocks:	handlebar mounted
Tank:	XLCR
Oil tank:	under seat
Seat:	race-style solo
Footrests:	footpegs
Electrics:	12-volt

PAINT AND FINISH

Paint:	HD
Colour:	black
Chrome/polish:	stock HD

Café Racer

The Café Racer was designed to combine road-race and flat-track race styling around a Sportster. The bike was not styled in the late 70s fashion of the Harley stock bikes and this factor meant it was not a big-seller in its day. In the late 90s, however, it is a collectable machine.

The XR1000 used the bottom end from the XL1000 Sportster with the cylinder heads from the racing XR750. A pair of race-type carbs were fitted to the right side of the engine.

The exhausts, unusually for a Harley-Davidson, both ran down the left side of the engine. This was necessitated by the fitting of the twin carburettors on the other side.

Apart from the engine, much of the XR1000 was stock Sportster, including the tachometer and speedometer mounted on a bracket from the handlebar clamps into the top fork yoke.

SPECIFICATION

1983 XR1000

Owner:	Motex Harley-Davidson Worcester, England

ENGINE

Model:	XR1000
Capacity:	61 cu in (1000 cc)
Cases:	HD
Carb:	twin carburettors
Air filter:	K&N
Ignition:	points
Pipes:	XR-750

TRANSMISSION

Type:	four speed

FRAME

Model:	swingarm XL

SUSPENSION

Front:	telescopic forks
Rear:	swingarm and shock absorbers

WHEELS AND BRAKES

Front:	19 in (48 cm) cast nine spoke
Brake:	twin discs
Rear:	16 in (41 cm) cast nine spoke
Brake:	single disc

FENDERS

Front:	XL
Rear:	XL

ACCESSORIES

Handlebars:	flat
Risers:	none
Headlight:	sealed beam
Tail-light:	stock HD
Clocks:	handlebar-mounted speedo/tacho
Tank:	Sportster
Oil tank:	under seat
Seat:	solo
Footrests:	footpegs
Electrics:	12-volt

PAINT AND FINISH

Paint:	HD
Colour:	orange and silver
Chrome/polish:	stock HD

1992 FXRS Convertible

Harley-Davidson's FXR Series Big Twin Evolution models were modern bikes with various factory-custom styling touches. In this range were the FXR Superglide, FXRS-SP Low Rider Sport, FXLR Low Rider Custom and the FXRS Convertible, as seen here.

All the FXR models feature rubber-mounted engines, five-speed transmission and final belt drives.

The result of this combination is a smooth, vibration-free motorcycle.

The FXRS Convertible is regarded as a versatile sport touring machine.

To make it suitable for touring it has refinements such as air-adjustable front suspension (through a chamber inside the handlebars), a removable Lexan windshield and removable saddlebags made from nylon and leather.

A Harley-Davidson sidecar can be fitted if required.

The model seen here has been further personalized by its owner who has incorporated a number of custom inspection and air cleaner covers as well as custom gas caps, a luggage rack and turn-signal ornaments.

1988 FLST Heritage Softail Classic

The Heritage Softail of 1988 was very much a 50s-inspired design based on the Harley-Davidson big twin motorcycle, but revamped for modern roads and traffic conditions and to appeal to the rapidly growing market for 'nostalgia' bikes.

It featured the Softail frame, which was a Harley-designed frame that looked like a traditional rigid frame but featured rear suspension to increase the rider and passenger's comfort.

This was done by adding a pivoted triangulated rear section to the frame in place of the more usual swinging arm.

The shock absorber for the new bike was underneath the frame. This kept the triangular lines of the frame clearly visible and although it is totally unlike pre-1958 Harley frames, the appearance is of a frame from this era.

The remainder of the bike was also styled in an old way, with large valanced FL fenders, studded saddlebags and saddle and a nostalgic two-tone paint scheme.

ble

FXRS Converti

The Heritage Softail featured forks that bore a strong resemblance to those from the 50s, with partially shrouded forks on which a large headlamp was mounted.

The nostalgic theme continues in the fenders by using fully valanced FL items painted in a two-tone paint scheme. The disc brake and caliper, however, are more up-to-date.

Twin filler caps, tank-mounted dash, wide bars and a view forward over the spotlights; from the rider's perspective the whole machine seems vintage rather than modern.

SPECIFICATION

1988 FLST Heritage Softail Classic

Owner:	Simon Winslow
	Swindon, England

ENGINE

Model:	Evolution
Capacity:	80 cu in (1340 cc)
Cases:	HD
Carb:	1.5 inch (38 mm) butterfly
Air filter:	S&S
Ignition:	electronic
Pipes:	staggered shorty duals

TRANSMISSION

Type:	five speed

FRAME

Model:	Softail FLST

SUSPENSION

Front:	telescopic forks
Rear:	Softail

WHEELS AND BRAKES

Front:	16 in (41 cm) spoked
Brake:	single disc
Rear:	16 in (41 cm) spoked
Brake:	disc

FENDERS

Front:	FL
Rear:	FL

ACCESSORIES

Handlebars:	wide flats
Risers:	none
Headlight:	9 in (23 cm) sealed beams
Tail-light:	stock HD
Clocks:	tank-mounted dash
Tank:	Fatbob
Oil tank:	chromed horseshoe
Seat:	solo saddle
Footrests:	footboards
Electrics:	12-volt

PAINT AND FINISH

Paint:	HD
Colour:	candy bronze and cream
Chrome/polish:	stock HD

Heritage Softail

The Heritage Softail was one of a number of bikes from Harley-Davidson that sold to those people interested in a 'nostalgia' motorcycle. Its styling is from the 50s and the bike's name reflects this.

The primary cover is so named because it covers the primary drive from the engine to the gearbox. This motorcycle has a custom clutch cover, inscribed 'live to ride, ride to live'.

The speedo and tachometer are mounted on the bars behind the windshield, with the fuel gauge and filler cap mounted in the raised dash panel – a variation on traditional Harley styling.

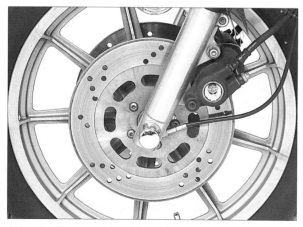

This is the standard braking set up for an FXRS, featuring twin discs – one on either side of the cast spoked wheel, with a hydraulically operated caliper for each disc on the fork leg.

SPECIFICATION

1992 FXRS Convertible

Owner:	Ron and Wendy Coles Swindon, England

ENGINE

Model:	Evolution
Capacity:	80 cu in (1340 cc)
Cases:	HD
Carb:	1.5 in (40 mm) CV
Air filter:	8 in (20 cm) circular chrome
Ignition:	electronic
Pipes:	staggered duals

TRANSMISSION

Type:	five speed

FRAME

Model:	Duplex cradle FXRS

SUSPENSION

Front:	telescopic forks
Rear:	swingarm and shock absorbers

WHEELS AND BRAKES

Front:	19 in (48 cm) cast alloy
Brake:	twin disks
Rear:	16 in (41 cm) cast alloy
Brake:	disc

FENDERS

Front:	stock HD
Rear:	stock HD

ACCESSORIES

Handlebars:	Buckhorn
Risers:	none
Headlight:	sealed beam
Tail-light:	stock HD
Clocks:	speedometer and tachometer
Tank:	4.2-gallon (15.9-litre) Fatbob
Oil tank:	3 quarts (2.8 litres)
Seat:	dual pillow seat
Footrests:	rubber isolated pegs
Electrics:	12-volt

PAINT AND FINISH

Paint:	HD
Colour:	two-tone victory red sun-glo
Chrome/polish:	black and chrome engine trim

1996 Electra Glide Standard FLHT

The Electra Glide has been in production since 1965 and sequentially updated.

This is the Electra Glide in its state-of-the-art 1996 form, refined and sophisticated but still a big touring motorcycle.

As a touring bike, the comfort of rider and pillion has been given main priority, not least in the size and depth of the seats and the fact that footboards are fitted for both people.

The engine is described as 'isolation-mounted' by Harley-Davidson to minimize vibration transmitted from the V-twin.

A fork-mounted fairing makes distance-riding more comfortable, as does the air suspension. To enable the occupants of the Electra Glide to travel and carry baggage, two large panniers are fitted, one either side of the rear fender, with a luggage rack over the same fender. This is also designed for load-carrying, either with a tour pack fitted as shown here or simply by strapping bags to the rack.

de

1995 FXDWG Dyna Wide Glide

Among the modifications added to this bike
are a raked out front end that is fitted with a
21 in (53 cm) front wheel, Apehanger
handlebars and a small front fender
complemented by a bobbed rear one.

These were, and still are, popular custom
modifications when building a custom Harley,
therefore Harley-Davidson decided to offer
their own version of a custom bike.

The customizing is slightly constrained
because, as a large company,
Harley-Davidson are legally
bound by legislation that does
not affect individual custom
builders. For example, a custom
builder may not fit a front fender but
the Harley-Davidson factory is
legally obliged to.

The Wide Glide designation refers
to the fact that the fork legs are
more widely spaced on this
model than on other big
twin Harleys.

Electra Glide

This custom rear fender originated from riders who cut down the large rear fenders on their bikes and moved them around the wheel. It reduced weight and was known as 'bobbing'.

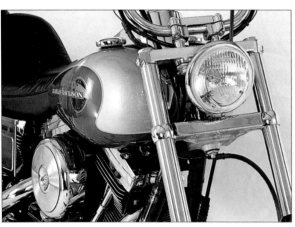

The Wide Glide name refers to the fact that the fork legs are wider on this model than on other Harleys in the range. This helps maintain the chopper style.

The large Apehanger bars give a distinctly chopper-like appearance to a stock production bike. Harley-Davidson were the first company to offer 'factory customs'.

SPECIFICATION

1995 FXDWG Dyna Wide Glide

Owner:	Mike Morse
	Swindon, England

ENGINE

Model:	Evolution
Capacity:	80 cu in (1340 cc)
Cases:	HD
Carb:	stock HD
Air filter:	8 in (20 cm) circular
Ignition:	electronic
Pipes:	staggered shorty duals

TRANSMISSION

Type:	five speed

FRAME

Model:	swingarm FXDWG

SUSPENSION

Front:	telescopic forks
Rear:	swingarm and shock absorbers

WHEELS AND BRAKES

Front:	21 in (53 cm) spoked
Brake:	single disc
Rear:	16 in (41 cm) spoked
Brake:	disc

FENDERS

Front:	sport
Rear:	bobtail

ACCESSORIES

Handlebars:	Apehangers
Risers:	none
Headlight:	chromed sealed beam
Tail-light:	stock HD
Clocks:	tank-mounted speedo
Tank:	Fatbob
Oil tank:	3 quarts (2.8 litres)
Seat:	stepped dual
Footrests:	forward controls
Electrics:	12-volt

PAINT AND FINISH

Paint:	HD
Colour:	two-tone aquamarine and silver
Chrome/polish:	stock HD

Dyna Wide Gli

This bike is a production model that can be described as a factory custom. Its origins are pure chopper, with the Harley designers producing their own interpretation of a modified stock bike.

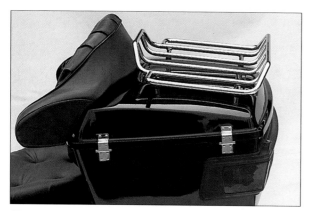

The tour pack comprises a cavernous box and pillion-passenger back rest that fixes to the luggage rack on the rear fender. It also incorporates turn signals.

The Evolution engine is rubber-mounted to reduce the vibration transmitted to the rider and passenger, both of whom are supplied with footboards to enhance comfort.

In a break from tradition, the instruments are mounted in the handlebar-mounted fairing rather than in the tank-mounted dash panel, which itself acts as the cover for the filler cap.

SPECIFICATION

1996 Electra Glide Standard FLHT

Owner:	Dale Richardson
	Greeley, Colorado

ENGINE

Model:	Evolution
Capacity:	80 cu in (1340 cc)
Cases:	HD
Carb:	HD stock
Air filter:	HD circular
Ignition:	electronic
Pipes:	two-into-one

TRANSMISSION

Type:	five speed

FRAME

Model:	swingarm FLH

SUSPENSION

Front:	telescopic forks
Rear:	swingarm and shock absorbers

WHEELS AND BRAKES

Front:	16 in (41 cm) cast 10 spoke
Brake:	twin discs
Rear:	16 in (41 cm) cast 10 spoke
Brake:	disc

FENDERS

Front:	stock FLHT
Rear:	stock FLHT

ACCESSORIES

Handlebars:	dresser
Risers:	none
Headlight:	6 in (15 cm) sealed beam
Tail-light:	stock HD
Clocks:	mounted in fairing
Tank:	Fatbob
Oil tank:	1 gallon (3.8 litres)
Seat:	dual
Footrests:	footboards
Electrics:	12-volt

PAINT AND FINISH

Paint:	HD
Colour:	vivid black
Chrome/polish:	stock HD

1996 FLSTC Heritage Classic

The FLSTC Heritage Softail Classic is a 'nostalgia' motorcycle. Its Hardtail frame styling is produced by the use of the Softail frame in conjunction with hydraulic telescopic front forks. It is in many ways the 50s Hydra Glide reincarnated for the 90s.

Unlike the Hydra Glide though, the Heritage Softail Classic features rear suspension and other refinements such as electric start, belt drive, front and rear disc brakes and the larger capacity Evolution V-twin.

Despite such modern components the styling is unmistakably big, old Harley-Davidson; the huge valanced FL fenders, shrouded forks on which the headlights, and windshield brackets are mounted, the wide dresser bars, timeless Fatbob tank that follows into a studded leather seat and the large studded saddlebags all contribute to this appearance.

The end result is the best of both worlds – modern convenience, comfort and speed and the style of an altogether different decade.

Electra Glide

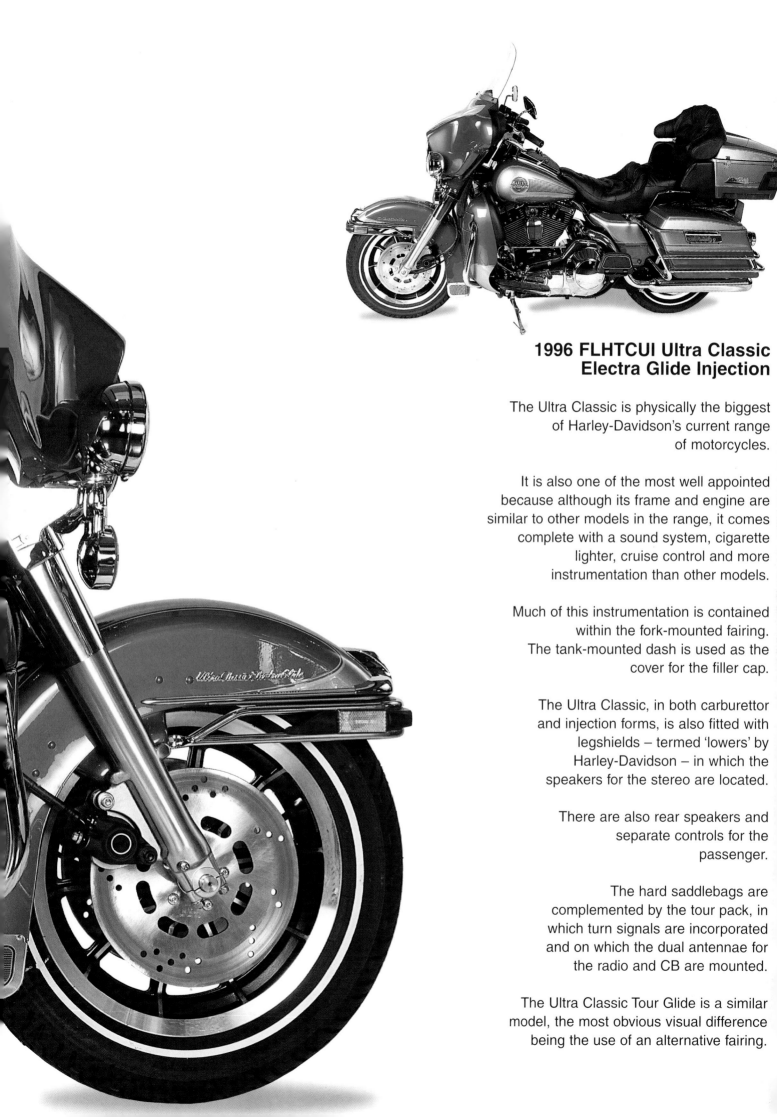

1996 FLHTCUI Ultra Classic Electra Glide Injection

The Ultra Classic is physically the biggest of Harley-Davidson's current range of motorcycles.

It is also one of the most well appointed because although its frame and engine are similar to other models in the range, it comes complete with a sound system, cigarette lighter, cruise control and more instrumentation than other models.

Much of this instrumentation is contained within the fork-mounted fairing. The tank-mounted dash is used as the cover for the filler cap.

The Ultra Classic, in both carburettor and injection forms, is also fitted with legshields – termed 'lowers' by Harley-Davidson – in which the speakers for the stereo are located.

There are also rear speakers and separate controls for the passenger.

The hard saddlebags are complemented by the tour pack, in which turn signals are incorporated and on which the dual antennae for the radio and CB are mounted.

The Ultra Classic Tour Glide is a similar model, the most obvious visual difference being the use of an alternative fairing.

ic

Heritage Class

The unusual feature on this Harley is that it uses fuel injection rather than the traditional carburettor. Harley-Davidson call their system Sequential Port Fuel Injection.

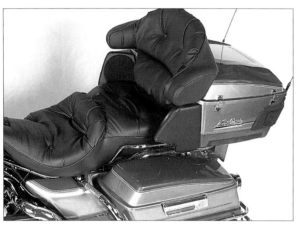

The Ultra Classic is intended for long-distance riding and as such provides as much comfort as possible for rider and passenger. The luxurious back rest is for the passenger.

The telescopic forks and twin-disc front brake, fitted to a 10-spoke alloy wheel, are considered sufficient to control the 765 lb (348 kg) bike.

SPECIFICATION

1996 FLHTCUI Ultra Classic Electra Glide Injection

Owner:	Motex Harley-Davidson Worcester, England

ENGINE

Model:	Evolution
Capacity:	80 cu in (1340 cc)
Cases:	HD
Carb:	fuel injection
Air filter:	8 in (20 cm) circular
Ignition:	electronic
Pipes:	dual system

TRANSMISSION

Type:	five speed

FRAME

Model:	swingarm FLHT

SUSPENSION

Front:	telescopic forks
Rear:	swingarm and shock absorbers

WHEELS AND BRAKES

Front:	16 in (41 cm) cast 10-spoke
Brake:	twin discs
Rear:	16 in (41 cm) cast 10-spoke
Brake:	disc

FENDERS

Front:	FL
Rear:	FL

ACCESSORIES

Handlebars:	dresser
Risers:	none
Headlight:	9 in (23 cm) sealed beam
Tail-light:	stock HD
Clocks:	fairing-mounted dash
Tank:	Fatbob
Oil tank:	1 gallon (3.8 litres)
Seat:	dual seat
Footrests:	footboards
Electrics:	12-volt

PAINT AND FINISH

Paint:	HD
Colour:	blue pearl
Chrome/polish:	stock HD

Ultra Classic

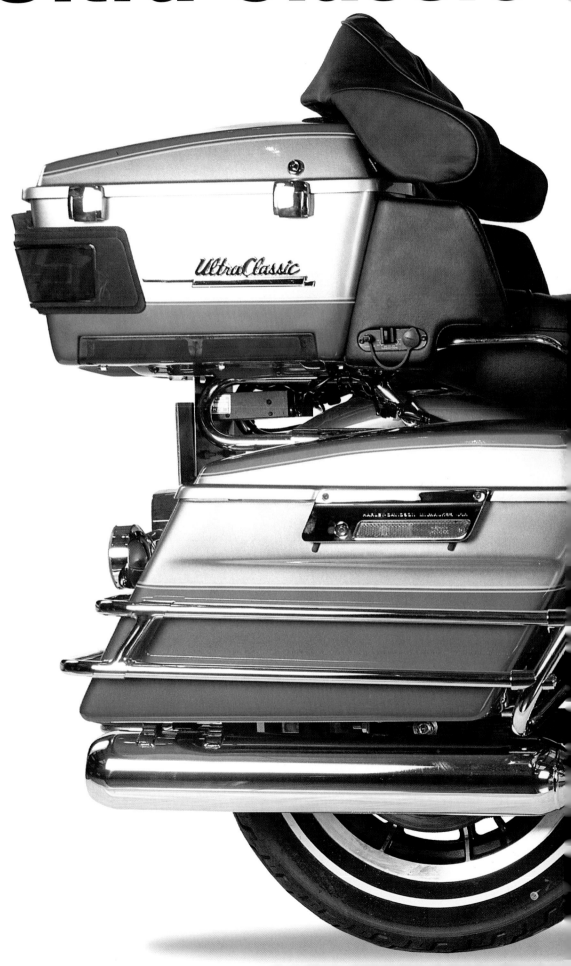

The front fender fitted to the FL models since the late 40s has been slightly modified to make it suitable for different forks and fender trims, but it has always kept the same shape.

The 50s styled saddlebags conceal much of the 90s Softail style rear suspension, ensuring the nostalgic look of the machine. The seat is similarly studded to maintain the style.

The spotlights (or passing lamps) mounted either side of the headlamp have long been a Harley-Davidson trademark, as has been mounting the turn signals below them.

SPECIFICATION

1996 FLSTC Heritage Classic

Owner:	Motex Harley-Davidson Worcester, England

ENGINE

Model:	Evolution
Capacity:	80 cu in (1340 cc)
Cases:	HD
Carb:	stock HD
Air filter:	8 in (20 cm) circular
Ignition:	electronic
Pipes:	staggered dual

TRANSMISSION

Type:	five speed

FRAME

Model:	Softail FLST

SUSPENSION

Front:	telescopic forks
Rear:	Softail

WHEELS AND BRAKES

Front:	16 in (41 cm) spoked
Brake:	single disc
Rear:	16 in (41 cm) spoked
Brake:	disc

FENDERS

Front:	FL
Rear:	FL

ACCESSORIES

Handlebars:	pullback
Risers:	none
Headlight:	9 in (23 cm) sealed beam
Tail-light:	stock HD
Clocks:	tank-mounted dash
Tank:	Fatbob
Oil tank:	3-quart (2.8-litre) horseshoe
Seat:	sprung solo saddle
Footrests:	footboards and pegs
Electrics:	12-volt

PAINT AND FINISH

Paint:	HD
Colour:	patriot red pearl
Chrome/polish:	stock HD

1996 FXDS Dyna Glide Convertible

The Dyna Glide frame was re-engineered for the 1996 models to create a lowered look. Although this is a traditional-looking bike, the FXDS Convertible is not as much of a nostalgia bike as several other models in the 90s range.

This is more of a dual-purpose bike – for both cruising and touring. The windshield and panniers are designed to be quickly removed to allow the motorcycle to switch roles.

The Evolution engine is rubber-mounted to minimize the vibration passed on to both rider and pillion passenger and other touring accessories include a pillion back rest.

The Dyna Convertible originated from the Super Glide, hence the FX prefix.

The Super Glide remains in the range as a basic and traditional big twin Harley, featuring the Dyna frame and Evolution engine, but with telescopic forks and spoked wheels.

Special

1996 FLSTN Heritage Softail Special

While the FLSTN features nostalgic items such as partially shrouded telescopic forks and 16 in (41 cm) whitewall tyres, it is not as much of a nostalgic dresser as the Heritage Softail Classic, but is nonetheless reminiscent of a slightly customized early 50s Hydra Glide.

The lines of the FL fenders are unmistakable and the Softail frame gives a rigid frame appearance – it takes more than a glance to spot the pivot for the rear portion of the frame (it is actually between the exhaust pipes behind the gearbox).

The chromed oil tank and two-tone paint give the custom appearance, as do the staggered dual exhaust pipes.

Fender trim, dash, running lights, turn signals, mirrors and headlight have all been updated, in some cases to conform to highway legislation and in others for appearance, but they remain in the Harley-Davidson style.

rtible

Dyna Glide Conv

The Dyna Glide frame was a logical progression from the 70s Super Glide, which is still produced as the FXD Super Glide. The FXD Dyna Glide Convertible is a dual purpose machine, as its 'convertible' name indicates.

The timeless FL front fender has updated trims and badges fitted; the front fender edge trim carries a version of the logo through which the running light lens shows.

The Fatbob tank carries the modern interpretation of the tank-mounted dash. The twin filler caps and two-tone paint are also traditional touches.

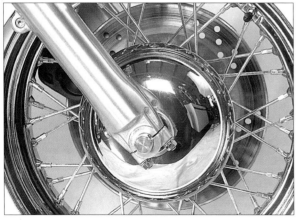

The 16 in (41 cm) spoked front wheel is fitted with a single disc brake rotor; the other side, seen here, has a hub cap fitted. Harley have made these components for several decades.

SPECIFICATION

1996 FLSTN Heritage Softail Special

Owner:	Motex Harley-Davidson Worcester, England

ENGINE

Model:	Evolution
Capacity:	80 cu in (1340 cc)
Cases:	HD
Carb:	stock HD
Air filter:	8 in (20 cm) circular
Ignition:	electronic
Pipes:	shotgun duals

TRANSMISSION

Type:	five speed

FRAME

Model:	Softail FLST

SUSPENSION

Front:	telescopic forks
Rear:	Softail

WHEELS AND BRAKES

Front:	16 in (41 cm) spoked
Brake:	single disc
Rear:	16 in (41 cm) spoked
Brake:	disc

FENDERS

Front:	FL
Rear:	FL

ACCESSORIES

Handlebars:	dresser
Risers:	none
Headlight:	9 in (23 cm) sealed beam
Tail-light:	stock HD
Clocks:	tank-mounted dash
Tank:	Fatbob
Oil tank:	3-quart (2.8-litre) horseshoe
Seat:	stepped dual
Footrests:	footboards
Electrics:	12-volt

PAINT AND FINISH

Paint:	HD
Colour:	two-tone mystique green and silver
Chrome/polish:	stock HD

Heritage Softail

This is another contemporary nostalgic Harley-Davidson based around the Softail frame and Evolution big twin engine.

The Dyna Glide's fork-mounted windshield can be easily removed, depending on whether the machine is being used for touring or cruising; the same applies to the saddlebags.

The Dyna Glide features a handlebar-mounted speedo and tacho, but retains the traditionally shaped Fatbob tank and dash. The dash houses the fuel gauge and filler cap.

Slender telescopic forks end at the hub of a 13-spoke cast alloy wheel, to which are bolted a pair of disc brake rotors. The calipers are bolted to the lower fork legs.

SPECIFICATION

1996 FXDS Dyna Glide Convertible

Owner:	Motex Harley-Davidson
	Worcester, England

ENGINE

Model:	Evolution
Capacity:	80 cu in (1340 cc)
Cases:	HD
Carb:	stock HD
Air filter:	8 in (20 cm) circular
Ignition:	electronic
Pipes:	staggered dual

TRANSMISSION

Type:	five speed

FRAME

Model:	swingarm FXDS

SUSPENSION

Front:	telescopic forks
Rear:	swingarm and shock absorbers

WHEELS AND BRAKES

Front:	19 in (48 cm) cast 13 spoke
Brake:	twin disc
Rear:	16 in (41 cm) cast 13 spoke
Brake:	disc

FENDERS

Front:	XL-type
Rear:	stock HD

ACCESSORIES

Handlebars:	pullback
Risers:	none
Headlight:	sealed beam
Tail-light:	stock HD
Clocks:	handlebar-mounted speedo/tacho
Tank:	Fatbob
Oil tank:	3 quarts (2.8 litres)
Seat:	dual
Footrests:	footpegs
Electrics:	12-volt

PAINT AND FINISH

Paint:	HD
Colour:	violet pearl
Chrome/polish:	stock HD

1996 FXSTSB Bad Boy

In some of their advertising copy Harley-Davidson mention that this bike has a notorious past. For example, the film, *The Wild One* was based on the alleged incidents in the town of Hollister, California after the Second World War. Many of the riders in Hollister rode bikes similar to those that the Bad Boy is now based upon.

Almost 50 years ago, riders rode bobbers, many of which featured shortened fenders, springer forks and a stripped down minimal look. The bikes they rode were based on Knuckleheads and Flatheads.

Harley, ever conscious of its history and heritage, introduced the Bad Boy based around a Softail frame and Evolution engine. The fenders are bobbed and the forks are springers and, like the bikes ridden in the 50s, this one also turns heads.

1996 FXSTS Softail Springer

In 1988 Harley-Davidson astounded the motorcycling world by reintroducing springer forks, which most people assumed had been consigned to the history books, having been completely superseded by telescopic forks.

Harley-Davidson had by then started marketing a significant percentage of their motorcycles as 'Nostalgia' bikes.

With this in mind, the reintroduction of components that had last been seen on their bikes in 1948 was a logical move.

The springer forks used on Evos have been updated from those used on Knuckleheads and Panheads and are now made with the assistance of computer-aided design and modern materials. They have also been fitted with a single disc brake.

The springer-forked motorcycles have now been in production again for eight years and are used on more than one model.

The Bad Boy, which is the nearest motorcycle to a factory-built chopper, is one of the models to use springers.

Bad Boy

The Bad Boy is Harley's most extreme factory custom to date and is in many ways more than a factory custom; it is a full factory chopper. As Harley-Davidson admit in some of their advertising, there is some notoriety in the history of these bikes.

The Softail Springer is a clever combination of the old and the new; here the vintage style springer fork and 21 in (53 cm) wheel is fitted with a modern disc brake and caliper.

The 'Nostalgia' headlamp is fixed high on the forks and, when seen in front of the Fatbob tank and buckhorn bars, conjures up images of earlier overhead-valve big twins.

The Softail frame was engineered to have the sleek appearance of a rigid frame but with the added advantage of suspension, thereby giving greater comfort to the rider and pillion.

SPECIFICATION

1996 FXSTS Softail Springer

Owner:	Gerry Stockwell
	Fairford, England

ENGINE

Model:	Evolution
Capacity:	80 cu in (1340 cc)
Cases:	HD
Carb:	HD
Air filter:	8 in (20 cm) circular
Ignition:	electronic
Pipes:	staggered shorty duals

TRANSMISSION

Type:	five speed

FRAME

Model:	Softail FXSTS

SUSPENSION

Front:	springer forks
Rear:	Softail

WHEELS AND BRAKES

Front:	21 in (53 cm) spoked
Brake:	single disc
Rear:	16 in (41 cm) spoked
Brake:	disc

FENDERS

Front:	springer
Rear:	bobbed

ACCESSORIES

Handlebars:	buckhorn
Risers:	yes
Headlight:	chrome bullet
Tail-light:	stock HD
Clocks:	tank-mounted dash
Tank:	Fatbob
Oil tank:	chromed horseshoe
Seat:	stepped dual
Footrests:	forward controls
Electrics:	12-volt

PAINT AND FINISH

Paint:	HD
Colour:	vivid black
Chrome/polish:	stock HD

Softail Springer

In 1947 Harley-Davidson introduced a hydraulic damper to control the movement of the springer forks in place of the hand adjusted 'ride control'. This was reintroduced on Softail Springers.

The Bad Boy is an interpretation of an old-time chopper; even the paint scheme follows this theme as scallops such as these, along with flames, were popular early custom paint jobs.

The scalloped paint work carries through onto the rear fender which in keeping with the style of the bike is bobbed, albeit fitted to a Softail frame.

SPECIFICATION

1996 FXSTSB Bad Boy

Owner:	Motex Harley-Davidson Worcester, England

ENGINE

Model:	Evolution
Capacity:	80 cu in (1340 cc)
Cases:	HD
Carb:	stock HD
Air filter:	8 in (20 cm) circular
Ignition:	electronic
Pipes:	staggered shorty duals

TRANSMISSION

Type:	five speed

FRAME

Model:	Softail FXST

SUSPENSION

Front:	springer forks
Rear:	softail

WHEELS AND BRAKES

Front:	21 in (53 cm) spoked
Brake:	single disc
Rear:	16 in (41 cm) slotted alloy
Brake:	disc

FENDERS

Front:	springer
Rear:	bobbed

ACCESSORIES

Handlebars:	pullbacks
Risers:	yes
Headlight:	chromed bullet
Tail-light:	stock HD
Clocks:	tank-mounted dash
Tank:	Fatbob
Oil tank:	painted horseshoe
Seat:	stepped dual
Footrests:	forward controls
Electrics:	12-volt

PAINT AND FINISH

Paint:	HD
Colour:	vivid black
Chrome/polish:	stock HD

1996 XL 1200S Sportster Sport

This nimble new model features a number of performance parts, such as gas-assisted rear shock absorbers and cartridge-type damper valving on the front forks, making the entire machine's suspension adjustable.

The front end also features twin floating disc brakes and a disc rear brake.

The styling reflects the bike's sporting aspirations; a pair of flat-track-style handlebars, the redesigned 3.3-gallon (12.5-litre) gas tank and a dual sports seat are complemented by the 13-spoke cast wheels.

The racing origins and performance aspect of the machine are underlined by the tank badge; the Harley-Davidson logo is prominent, as is a V logo, referring to the legendary V-twin. A panel of race-style chequers completes the design.

1996 FLSTF Fat Boy

The Fat Boy caused a stir on its introduction, not least because of its unusual name but also because of its appearance. A factory custom from a completely different mould, the Fat Boy, with its squat stance and solid cast-alloy wheels, was a heavyweight, solid motorcycle.

The first models were only available in grey but since then the Fat Boy has become a regular in the Harley-Davidson range and is now sold in a number of different colours.

The FLSTF Fat Boy somehow projects an old-style look while being completely modern: its overall shape may be almost vintage but its solid wheels, Evolution engine and custom-style parts, which include the front fender and shotgun dual exhaust pipes, are up-to-date. The model has been slightly upgraded each year.

Harley followed the Fat Boy with another unusually named machine, the Bad Boy, and have introduced a new vintage style model for 1997 which is known as the Old Boy.

1200S Sportste

The success of the various Sportster circuit-racing series around the
world and the proven dirt- and flat-track heritage of the Sportster
caused Harley-Davidson to bring out a new model in 1996. It was the
XL 1200S Sportster Sport.

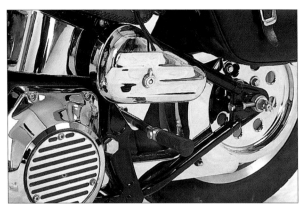

The teardrop-shaped toolbox has been fitted to Harley-Davidsons since before WWII. Also shown is the chromed horseshoe oil tank, which curves around the battery.

The air cleaner is made from chromed steel and fitted with a spun aluminium centre insert. In 1993 the engine breather system was redesigned to eliminate the pipes to this filter.

Both the wheels are cast from alloy and are 16 in (41 cm) in diameter. The hub is drilled to accept standard Harley components such as brake rotors, belt drive pulleys and axles.

SPECIFICATION

1996 FLSTF Fat Boy

Owner:	Robert Ashman
	Swindon, England

ENGINE

Model:	Evolution
Capacity:	80 cu in (1340 cc)
Cases:	HD
Carb:	HD stock
Air filter:	HD stock
Ignition:	electronic
Pipes:	shotgun duals

TRANSMISSION

Type:	five speed

FRAME

Model:	Softail FLSTF

SUSPENSION

Front:	telescopic forks
Rear:	Softail and shock absorber

WHEELS AND BRAKES

Front:	16 in (41 cm) solid alloy
Brake:	single drum
Rear:	16 in (41 cm) solid alloy
Brake:	disc

FENDERS

Front:	stock HD
Rear:	stock HD

ACCESSORIES

Handlebars:	wide FLH style
Risers:	aluminium clamp
Headlight:	sealed beam
Tail-light:	stock HD
Clocks:	tank-mounted dash
Tank:	Fatbob
Oil tank:	chromed horseshoe
Seat:	solo saddle and removable pillion
Footrests:	footboards
Electrics:	12-volt

PAINT AND FINISH

Paint:	HD
Colour:	two-tone wineberry sun-glo
Chrome/polish:	HD

Fat Boy

The up-and-down movement of the swingarm is controlled by the use of gas-assisted rear shocks. The rear disc is full-floating and bolted to the hub of the 13-spoke cast alloy wheel.

The tank badge features three parts – the maker's name, a V logo to emphasize the engine type and a panel of race-type chequers to indicate the Sportster's competitive history.

The racetrack-oval-inspired air cleaner is of chromed steel but fitted with an aluminium insert that indicates the metric capacity of the Sportster's engine, an Evolution unit.

SPECIFICATION

1996 XL 1200S Sportster Sport

Owner:	Motex Harley-Davidson Worcester, England

ENGINE

Model:	Evolution
Capacity:	73 cu in (1200 cc)
Cases:	HD
Carb:	stock HD
Air filter:	racetrack oval
Ignition:	electronic
Pipes:	staggered dual

TRANSMISSION

Type:	five speed

FRAME

Model:	swingarm XL

SUSPENSION

Front:	telescopic forks
Rear:	swingarm and shock absorbers

WHEELS AND BRAKES

Front:	19 in (48 cm) cast 13-spoke
Brake:	twin disc
Rear:	16 in (41 cm) cast 13-spoke
Brake:	disc

FENDERS

Front:	XL
Rear:	XL

ACCESSORIES

Handlebars:	flat track
Risers:	aluminium
Headlight:	sealed beam
Tail-light:	stock HD
Clocks:	handlebar-mounted speedo/tacho
Tank:	3.3-gallon (12.5-litre) Sportster
Oil tank:	3 quarts (2.8 litres)
Seat:	dual sport
Footrests:	footpegs
Electrics:	12-volt

PAINT AND FINISH

Paint:	HD
Colour:	two-tone violet and red pearl
Chrome/polish:	stock HD

1996 XL Sportster 1200 Custom

Harley-Davidson, aware of the heritage of the smaller capacity Sportster models, introduced the 1200 Custom as a new addition to their 1996 range.

The redesigned model enhances the Sportster's lean lines.

The suspension was lowered and a redesigned 3.3-gallon (12.5-litre) gas tank, new emblem and custom-style seat were all fitted.

Also selected to give a custom appearance were the chromed bullet headlight, low-rise handlebars and tall risers. The controls on the handlebars are less cluttered than on models from previous years and more of the wiring has been hidden.

A 21 in (53 cm) front wheel and 16 in (41 cm) rear are standard custom fare, although in true 90s style the front is spoked, while the rear is of a tough slotted alloy design.

Belt drive and disc brakes round the Sportster off mechanically and a selection of paint schemes complete the machine's appearance.

This Sportster Custom is finished in two-tone platinum silver and black.

1996 XLH Sportster Hugger

The 883 Sportster has the smallest displacement of any motorcycle in the Harley-Davidson range – 53.9 cu in; the 883 designation refers to its displacement in cubic centimetres. It is also the smallest model in the range in terms of weight and length.

The 883 is one of a number of Sportster models in a range that includes 73 cu in (1200 cc) bikes.

The Sportster is a traditional motorcycle that has been sequentially upgraded through its long production run.

This 1996 model is powered by the proven Evolution V2 engine, with a five-speed transmission and belt final drive. The latter feature was newly introduced in 1993.

There are race events around the world for the 883 Sportsters on both surfaced and unsurfaced tracks; the 883 is used as the basis for dirt-track race bikes as well as a series of surfaced-track races (like the US Twinsports) exclusive to 883 Sportsters.

Custom

Sportster 1200

The XL Sportster was first introduced in 1957. Four decades later Harley-Davidson are still making a motorcycle with the same name although everything about the machine has been altered.

The 883 Evolution Sportster engine is the smallest in the Harley-Davidson range and is a 'unit' construction – the engine and gearbox are assembled in one single casting.

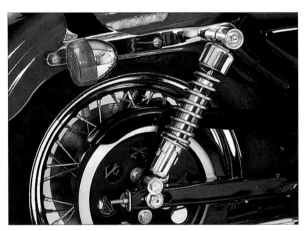

The belt final drive is seen here around the rear pulley. Belt drives give a smoother ride, especially when coupled with swingarm suspension and rear shock absorbers.

Unlike the larger capacity Harleys, the Sportster has a small gas tank which, when coupled with buckhorn handlebars and handlebar-mounted clocks, gives a unique appearance.

SPECIFICATION

1996 XLH Sportster Hugger

Owner:	Jeremy Griffin
	Eastleigh, England

ENGINE

Model:	Evolution
Capacity:	54 cu in (883 cc)
Cases:	HD
Carb:	1.5 in (40 mm) CV
Air filter:	oval racetrack
Ignition:	electronic
Pipes:	staggered duals

TRANSMISSION

Type:	five speed/belt drive

FRAME

Model:	Duplex cradle Sportster

SUSPENSION

Front:	telescopic forks
Rear:	swingarm and shock absorbers

WHEELS AND BRAKES

Front:	19 in (48 cm) spoked
Brake:	single disc
Rear:	16 in (41 cm) spoked
Brake:	disc

FENDERS

Front:	standard Sportster
Rear:	standard Sportster

ACCESSORIES

Handlebars:	Buckhorn
Risers:	none
Headlight:	sealed beam
Tail-light:	stock HD
Clocks:	speedometer and tachometer
Tank:	2.25-gallon (8.5-litre) Sportster
Oil tank:	3 quarts (2.8 litres)
Seat:	dual seat
Footrests:	rubber-mounted
Electrics:	12-volt

PAINT AND FINISH

Paint:	stock HD
Colour:	scarlet red
Chrome/polish:	polished engine trim

Sportster Hugger

The long-running Sportster tank has been redesigned for the new 1996 1200 Custom model and now features a narrower design and a redesigned emblem.

The windshield is an accessory on this Sportster but the low-rise handlebars are part of the custom package offered as standard with this new variant of the 1200 Sportster.

Both 883 and 1200 Sportsters are of unit construction, where the engine crankcase and gearbox housing are cast as one component. On big twins these are separate components.

SPECIFICATION

1996 XL Sportster 1200 Custom

Owner:	Chris Parry
	Swindon, England

ENGINE

Model:	Evolution
Capacity:	74 cu in (1200 cc)
Cases:	HD
Carb:	HD
Air filter:	racetrack oval
Ignition:	electronic
Pipes:	staggered shorty duals

TRANSMISSION

Type:	five speed

FRAME

Model:	swingarm Sportster

SUSPENSION

Front:	telescopic forks
Rear:	swingarm and shock absorbers

WHEELS AND BRAKES

Front:	21 in (53 cm) spoked
Brake:	single disc
Rear:	16 in (41 cm) slotted alloy
Brake:	disc

FENDERS

Front:	Sportster
Rear:	Sportster

ACCESSORIES

Handlebars:	low rise
Risers:	yes
Headlight:	chrome bullet
Tail-light:	stock HD
Clocks:	handlebar-mounted speedo
Tank:	3.3-gallon (12.5-litre) Sportster
Oil tank:	3 quarts (2.8 litres)
Seat:	stepped dual
Footrests:	footpegs
Electrics:	12-volt

PAINT AND FINISH

Paint:	HD
Colour:	two-tone platinum silver and black
Chrome/polish:	stock HD

1995 Custom Shovelhead

Customized Harley-Davidsons such as this are referred to as Lowriders because their styling is designed to be long and low. The standard Harley frame is modified to give it these attributes; the frame is made to ride lower in a variety of ways, including reducing the length of the rear shock absorbers and front forks and altering the rake of the forks, which lengthens and lowers the machine.

Once the frame modifications have been done the lowered look is enhanced through the use of modified fuel tanks and fenders and by fitting appropriate parts such as the custom seat.

1996 FXSTC Softail Custom

Harley-Davidson have always looked at what custom builders do to their products and then offered their own interpretation of the style. The customizing is slightly constrained because, as a company, Harley-Davidson are legally bound by legislation that does not affect individual custom builders. Nevertheless, Harley-Davidson offers acceptably styled factory customs.

The 1996 Softail Custom is this type of bike; it looks like a neatly customized bike rather than an ordinary stock bike.

The bike is based around the Softail frame which offers Hardtail styling with the benefit of rear suspension.

A bobbed rear fender, stepped seat, Fatbob tank, raked out front end, forward control pegs and foot pedals, a minimal front fender and big pullback bars are all the definitive after-market parts necessary to build a custom big twin.

The solid alloy rear wheel is a more modern custom-style part.

Harley-Davidson have collected these parts, assembled them around a Big Twin Evolution engine and five-speed transmission, and offer the custom bike straight off the dealer's showroom floor.

ead

Custom Shovelhe

This lowrider has been constructed around a frame modified to lower the whole motorcycle. It uses a Shovelhead engine and numerous after-market custom parts. It is finished with a one-off custom paint job.

From this angle, the factory FXSTC looks distinctly chopped; its pullback bars on risers from the 'wide glide' front end flow into the big Fatbob tank and on into the stepped seat.

The polished fork yokes, with a small custom-style headlamp, bear a close resemblance to the parts developed by custom bike builders before the concept of the factory custom was established.

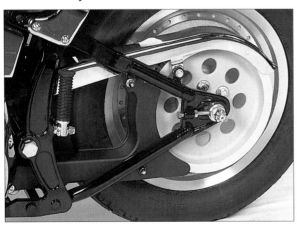

The Softail frame looks like the rigid frames last used in some of their Panhead models. The belt drive is concealed behind the guard in front of the 16 in (41 cm) cast alloy wheel.

SPECIFICATION

1996 FXSTC Softail Custom

Owner:	Motex Harley-Davidson Worcester, England

ENGINE

Model:	Evolution
Capacity:	80 cu in (1340 cc)
Cases:	HD
Carb:	stock HD
Air filter:	8 in (20 cm) circular
Ignition:	electronic
Pipes:	staggered shorty duals

TRANSMISSION

Type:	five speed

FRAME

Model:	Softail FXST

SUSPENSION

Front:	telescopic forks
Rear:	Softail

WHEELS AND BRAKES

Front:	21 in (53 cm) spoked
Brake:	single disc
Rear:	16 in (41 cm) alloy
Brake:	disc

FENDERS

Front:	XL type
Rear:	bobbed

ACCESSORIES

Handlebars:	pullbacks
Risers:	pullback
Headlight:	chromed sealed beam
Tail-light:	stock HD
Clocks:	tank-mounted dash
Tank:	Fatbob
Oil tank:	3-quart (2.8-litre) horseshoe
Seat:	stepped dual
Footrests:	forward controls
Electrics:	12-volt

PAINT AND FINISH

Paint:	HD
Colour:	patriot red pearl
Chrome/polish:	stock HD

Softail Custom

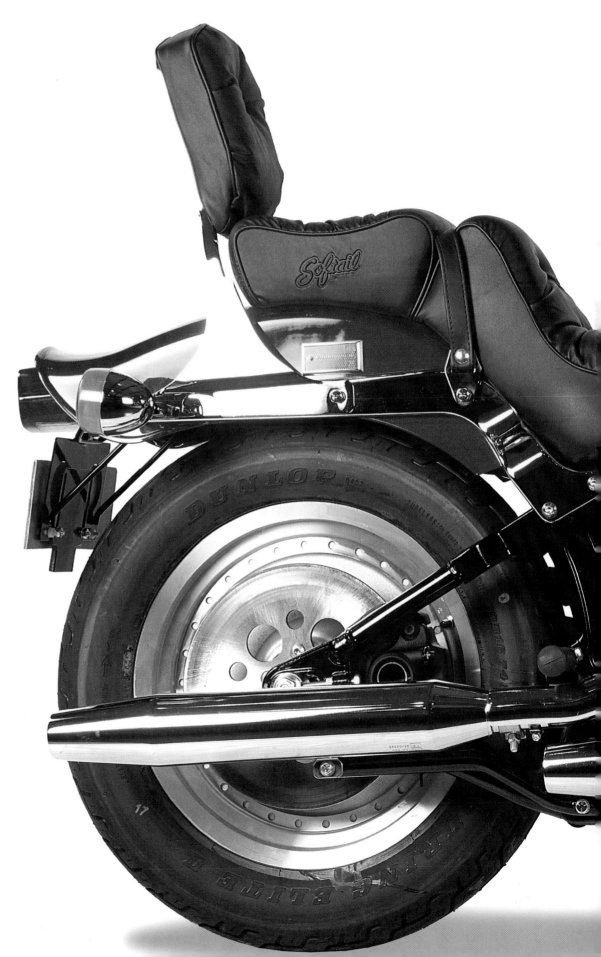

Each component on a custom Harley is carefully chosen and polished or painted. Here the rear brake disc and caliper have been fitted on a custom 16 in (41 cm) rear wheel.

S&S (Smith and Smith) are a renowned US performance-component manufacturer, particularly noted for carburettors and these distinctive air cleaner covers.

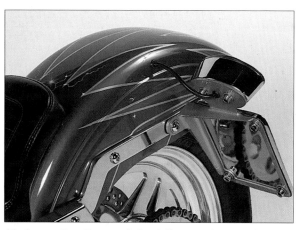

To keep the lines of the bike uncluttered the number of brackets are kept to a minimum. Here the licence plate bracket also carries the tail-light and is fixed to the rear fender strut.

SPECIFICATION

1995 Custom Shovelhead

Owner:	Airbrush Willie
	Genk, Belgium

ENGINE

Model:	Shovelhead
Capacity:	80 cu in (1340 cc)
Cases:	HD
Carb:	S&S Super
Air filter:	S&S Teardrop
Ignition:	points
Pipes:	BUB Bad Dog

TRANSMISSION

Type:	four speed

FRAME

Model:	swingarm Shovelhead

SUSPENSION

Front:	telescopic forks
Rear:	swingarm and shock absorbers

WHEELS AND BRAKES

Front:	21 in (53 cm) custom five-spoke
Brake:	twin Performance Machine discs
Rear:	16 in (41 cm) custom five-spoke
Brake:	PM disc and caliper

FENDERS

Front:	custom
Rear:	modified HD

ACCESSORIES

Handlebars:	pullback drags
Risers:	integral with triple tree
Headlight:	Bates
Tail-light:	cat's eye
Clocks:	tank mounted
Tank:	custom Fatbob
Oil tank:	HD
Seat:	custom solo
Footrests:	forward controls
Electrics:	12-volt

PAINT AND FINISH

Paint:	Airbrush Willie
Colour:	custom graphics
Chrome/polish:	alloy parts

Custom Lowrider

This type of custom bike is known as a Lowrider as it indicates its low profile, which is emphasized by the length of the bike. In order to build such a custom Harley, extensive frame modifications must be made or a custom-made frame purchased.

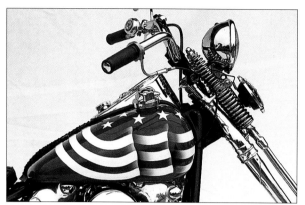

The classic lines of early choppers are seen here where the raked forks angle away from the frame, the headlight is mounted high above the springers, and risers carry the handlebars.

The secret to a neat-looking chopper is uncluttered lines, like this tall, graceful spoked rim laced to the stock star hub and with no front brake. The dice is another custom touch.

The chromed engine components dress up what is one of the last Knucklehead engines made; they were discontinued in 1948, the year after this one was built.

SPECIFICATION

1947 Knucklehead Chopper

Owner:	Dale Richardson
	Greeley, Colorado

ENGINE

Model:	Knucklehead
Capacity:	74 cu in (1200 cc)
Cases:	HD
Carb:	stock
Air filter:	circular chrome
Ignition:	points
Pipes:	drag pipes

TRANSMISSION

Type:	four speed

FRAME

Model:	HD rigid straightleg modified

SUSPENSION

Front:	6 in (15 cm) extended springer forks
Rear:	none

WHEELS AND BRAKES

Front:	21 in (53 cm) spoked
Brake:	none
Rear:	16 in (41 cm) spoked
Brake:	drum

FENDERS

Front:	none
Rear:	bobbed flat

ACCESSORIES

Handlebars:	dresser
Risers:	dogbone
Headlight:	Bates
Tail-light:	cat's eye
Clocks:	dash-mounted speedo
Tank:	Fatbob
Oil tank:	horseshoe
Seat:	king and queen
Footrests:	footboards and pegs
Electrics:	six-volt

PAINT AND FINISH

Paint:	custom stars and stripes
Colour:	red, white and blue
Chrome/polish:	chromed parts

1947 Knucklehead Chopper

This bike is sure to conjure up images of *Easyrider* and *Captain America*.

While the *Captain America* bike was powered by a Panhead engine, it came from the same school of design as this classic chopper, with its timeless lines and Knucklehead engine.

The bike was originally built in the 60s but restored in the 90s – a truly classic custom.

It was first built in the years before the widespread availability of an almost endless selection of custom parts and so used a mixture of both standard and modified parts.

Parts used in this type of bike included a straightleg rigid Harley frame, extended stock springer forks and a minimal rear fender.

The angle of the headstock was modified to allow the fitment of the overlong forks and certain components such as the front brake and fender were deliberately omitted while the machine was being assembled.

1995 FXRSS Custom Lowrider

Many early Harley-Davidson Lowriders used Sportster engines and transmissions because the compact size of the combined unit meant it was possible to build a machine that was long, low and elegant.

This machine has these attributes, despite using a big twin Evolution engine and gearbox.

So many custom parts have been used in this bike's construction by the English custom bike shop, Battistini's Custom Cycles, that little of it actually came from the Harley-Davidson factory.

Many of the parts used have come from specialist after-market manufacturers, such as the Californian Arlen Ness.

Knucklehead Chopper

The engine and transmission of this Lowrider have been reconstructed using a number of specialist billet alloy parts. This includes the primary drive and ignition coil covers.

The performance brakes and styling are complemented by a streamlined custom gas tank and mini fairing, with a tinted windscreen from which the handlebars curve backwards.

Every part of this bike has been modified in some way, including the triangular side panel which fits into the frame either side of the oil tank. It now fits the redesigned frame.

SPECIFICATION

1995 FXRSS Custom Lowrider

Owner:	Battistini's Custom Cycles
	Bournemouth, England

ENGINE

Model:	Evolution
Capacity:	80 cu in (1340 cc)
Cases:	HD
Carb:	S&S
Air filter:	none
Ignition:	electronic
Pipes:	custom

TRANSMISSION

Type:	five speed

FRAME

Model:	swingarm custom

SUSPENSION

Front:	telescopic forks
Rear:	custom swingarm/shock absorbers

WHEELS AND BRAKES

Front:	19 in (48 cm) spoked
Brake:	twin discs
Rear:	18 in (46 cm) spoked
Brake:	disc

FENDERS

Front:	custom
Rear:	custom

ACCESSORIES

Handlebars:	pullback drag
Risers:	integral with bars
Headlight:	fairing-mounted sealed beam
Tail-light:	cat's eye
Clocks:	handlebar-mounted speedo
Tank:	custom
Oil tank:	under seat
Seat:	custom solo
Footrests:	forward controls
Electrics:	12-volt

PAINT AND FINISH

Paint:	Battistini's
Colour:	custom two-tone
Chrome/polish:	custom billet aluminium

1995 Twin Supercharged Harman

The forks on this custom bike are from a Suzuki GSX-R1100 but have been modified in keeping with the rest of the bike. The brakes are high-tech and feature no less than four Harrison-billet six-piston calipers on the front; two on each disc. The rear brakes feature a pair of the same calipers on the disc.

The complex engine assembly has been fitted into a heavily modified frame. This has been complemented by one-off gas tank, seat and fenders, all made by Dave Batchelor at P&D in Sussex, England.

The custom paint and chroming were carried out before this stunning custom Harley was considered finished.

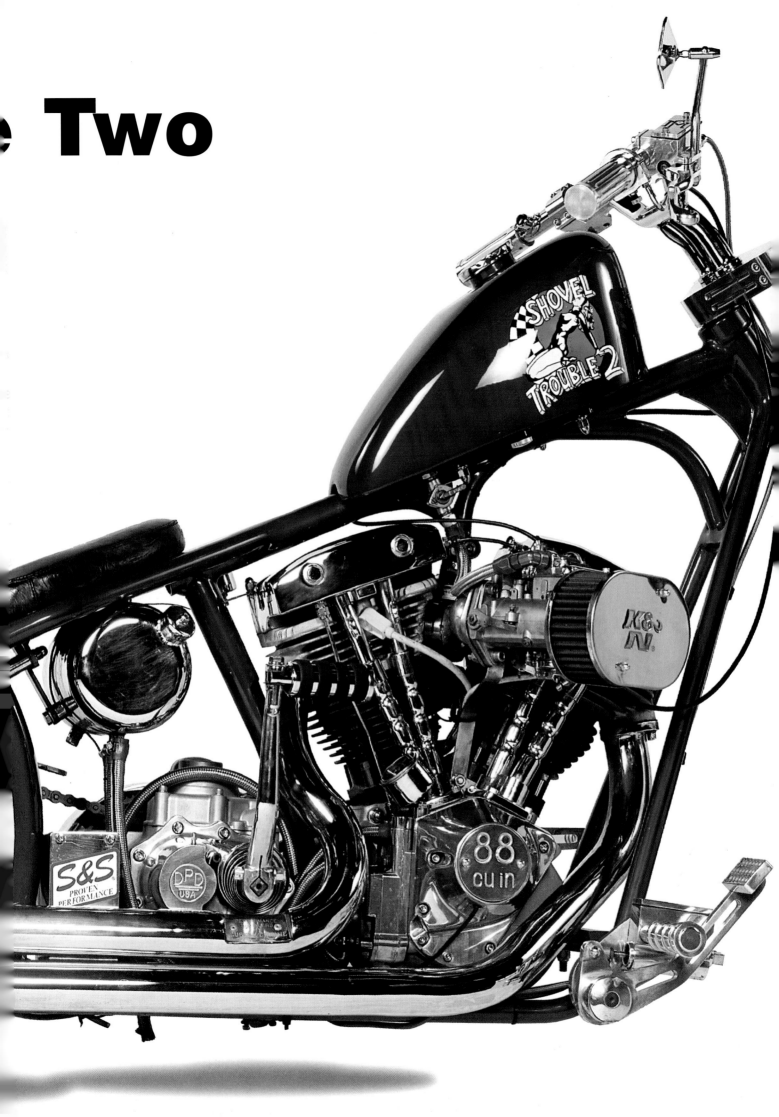

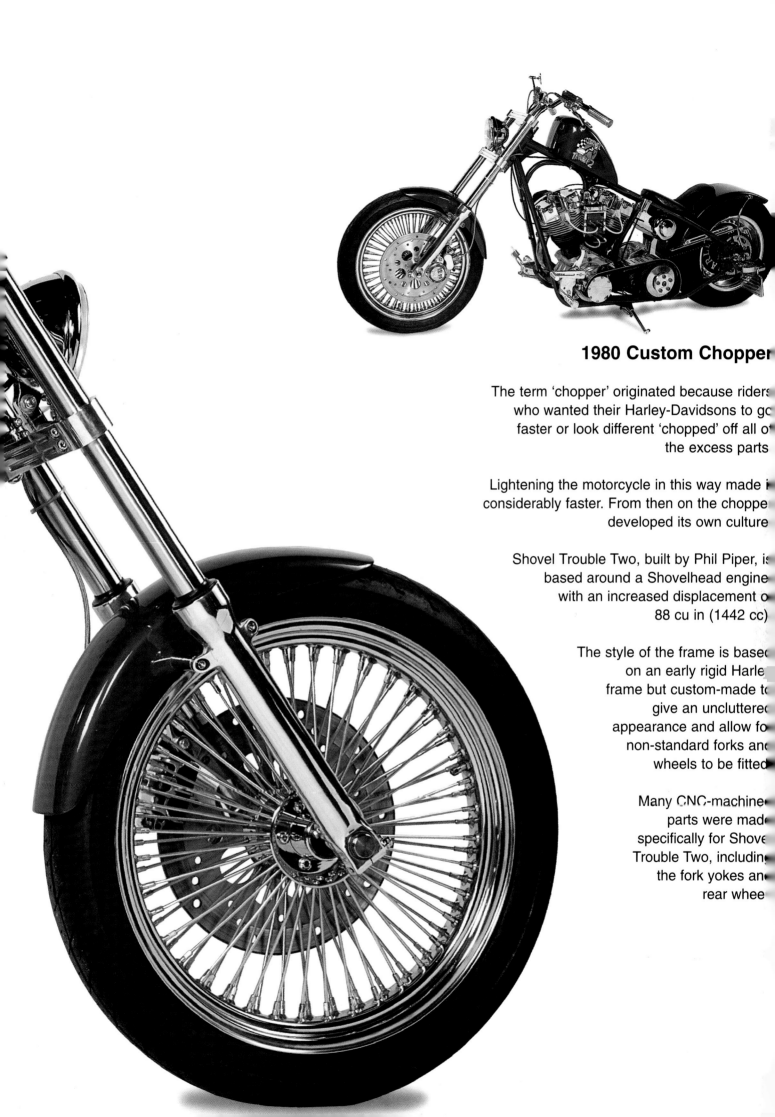

Two

1980 Custom Chopper

The term 'chopper' originated because riders who wanted their Harley-Davidsons to go faster or look different 'chopped' off all of the excess parts

Lightening the motorcycle in this way made it considerably faster. From then on the chopper developed its own culture

Shovel Trouble Two, built by Phil Piper, is based around a Shovelhead engine with an increased displacement of 88 cu in (1442 cc)

The style of the frame is based on an early rigid Harley frame but custom-made to give an uncluttered appearance and allow for non-standard forks and wheels to be fitted

Many CNC-machined parts were made specifically for Shovel Trouble Two, including the fork yokes and rear wheel

Twin Supercharge

This motorcycle is an example of custom and performance engineering at its most extreme. The engine, a 1988 Harman, features two superchargers which required a vast amount of specialist machining. Manifolds and drive pulleys were fabricated and geared to make the superchargers run at the engine-to-blower ratio of 1:1.

To keep a chopper looking minimal, a gas tank from the Sportster models is often used in place of a larger Harley gas tank. Here the tank has been custom airbrushed.

A modern custom touch is to have traditional spoked wheels built for a chopper with more than the normal 40 spokes. This wheel has 80 spokes assembled in an unusual lacing pattern.

The Shovelhead engine has been greatly modified, as has the ignition system. Each cylinder head has two plugs to ensure more even combustion.

SPECIFICATION

1980 Custom Chopper

| Owner: | Phil Piper |
| | Leicester, England |

ENGINE

Model:	Shovelhead
Capacity:	88 cu in (1442 cc)
Cases:	HD
Carb:	Dell'Orto
Air filter:	K&N
Ignition:	Accel
Pipes:	one-off

TRANSMISSION

Type:	four speed

FRAME

Model:	rigid custom-made

SUSPENSION

Front:	telescopic forks
Rear:	none

WHEELS AND BRAKES

Front:	21 in (53 cm) spoked
Brake:	disc
Rear:	15 in (38 cm) solid
Brake:	disc

FENDERS

Front:	custom
Rear:	custom

ACCESSORIES

Handlebars:	pullbacks
Risers:	integral with handlebars
Headlight:	Bates
Tail-light:	cat's eye
Clocks:	frame-mounted speedo
Tank:	Sportster
Oil tank:	custom
Seat:	custom solo
Footrests:	forward controls
Electrics:	12-volt

PAINT AND FINISH

Paint:	custom
Colour:	one-off mix
Chrome/polish:	custom as required

Shovel Troubl

This chopper is a modern version of a traditional Harley chopper.
It uses a rigid frame, Shovelhead engine and over-length forks with
a plethora of modern parts.

The carburettors were fitted to the superchargers and were attached to the engine through specially machined manifolds. The supercharger drive was built from scratch.

The rear fender is an unusual shape and almost completely hides the Metzeler rear tyre, although the wheel and complex brace assembly are clearly visible.

The front fender mirrors the rear and was made to fit the modified Suzuki forks, with twin six-piston brake calipers on each fork leg giving massive braking capability.

SPECIFICATION

1995 Twin Supercharged Harman

Owner:	Richard Taylor
	Kent, England

ENGINE

Model:	Harman
Capacity:	120 cu in (2000 cc)
Cases:	Harman
Carb:	twin 2 in (45 mm) Dell'Orto
Air filter:	twin K&N
Ignition:	Crane HI-4
Pipes:	one-off

TRANSMISSION

Type:	four speed

FRAME

Model:	swingarm P&D modified HD

SUSPENSION

Front:	telescopic forks
Rear:	swingarm and shock absorbers

WHEELS AND BRAKES

Front:	19 in (48 cm) spoked
Brake:	twin discs
Rear:	18 in (46 cm) spoked
Brake:	disc

FENDERS

Front:	handmade
Rear:	handmade

ACCESSORIES

Handlebars:	handmade
Risers:	billet
Headlight:	handmade
Tail-light:	twin cat's eyes
Clocks:	custom mini
Tank:	P&D custom
Oil tank:	handmade
Seat:	P&D solo
Footrests:	handmade
Electrics:	12-volt

PAINT AND FINISH

Paint:	Matt the Painter
Colour:	deep cherry red
Chrome/polish:	London Chroming

1995 Custom Lowrider Evo

This contemporary bike was built by the Dutch specialists O.I.T., whose principal aim was to build a performance-styled machine with sleek lines and up-rated chassis components.

This has been achieved through the use of upside-down forks and modified brake discs and calipers. Numerous billet aluminium parts, such as master cylinders, handlebar grips and engine components, are also included.

The wheels have been fitted with large tyres and the fenders chosen to be as minimal as possible. The tank has been modified to suit the lines of the frame and the whole machine is finished with custom graphics. The cylinder barrels have been painted to match the rest of the bike.

1993 Twin Dell'Orto

Most of the customizing was carried out by Classic and Custom Motorcycles at Chesterfield. Other specialists were engaged to fit the computer-controlled nitrous oxide system to the engine; this is a drag-race inspired performance modification, with a nitrous bottle on each side of the rear fender to supply each of the carburettors.

The engine was rebuilt to suit such a modification and performance exhaust pipes were also added.

The remainder of the bike was redesigned to emphasize its long, low lines and after-market wheels and brakes were fitted before a custom painter was engaged to spray the graphics that flow down the bike.

Lowrider Evo

The rider's eye view of this symmetrical custom bike shows the twin performance carburettors, pullback handlebars and custom oval rear-view mirrors.

One of the nitrous oxide bottles is bolted to the rear fender struts. The cat's eye tail-light has been fitted with a favourite custom 'blue dot'; a small faceted blue lens.

The triangular Softail portion of the frame has been chromed and a billet brake caliper added to the stock Harley brake disc, itself bolted to the Revtech custom rear wheel.

SPECIFICATION

1993 Twin Dell'Orto

Owner:	Chris Butler
	Chesterfield, England

ENGINE

Model:	Evolution
Capacity:	80 cu in (1340 cc)
Cases:	HD
Carb:	twin Dell'Orto
Air filter:	twin K&N
Ignition:	electronic
Pipes:	porker

TRANSMISSION

Type:	five speed

FRAME

Model:	Softail FXSTC

SUSPENSION

Front:	telescopic forks
Rear:	HD Softail

WHEELS AND BRAKES

Front:	21 in (53 cm) alloy
Brake:	single disc
Rear:	19 in (48 cm) alloy
Brake:	disc

FENDERS

Front:	Arlen Ness custom
Rear:	HD Fatbob

ACCESSORIES

Handlebars:	drag bars
Risers:	integral with bars
Headlight:	custom sealed beam
Tail-light:	cat's eye with blue dot
Clocks:	tank-mounted dash
Tank:	Fatbob
Oil tank:	stock HD chromed
Seat:	solo custom
Footrests:	PM forwards
Electrics:	12-volt

PAINT AND FINISH

Paint:	John Spurgeon
Colour:	one-off
Chrome/polish:	custom parts in alloy and chrome

Twin Dell'Orto

Chris Butler started out with an almost standard Softail that he purchased with a view to building a head-turning custom machine. He decided on the style of custom bike he wanted and commissioned specialist companies to carry out the work.

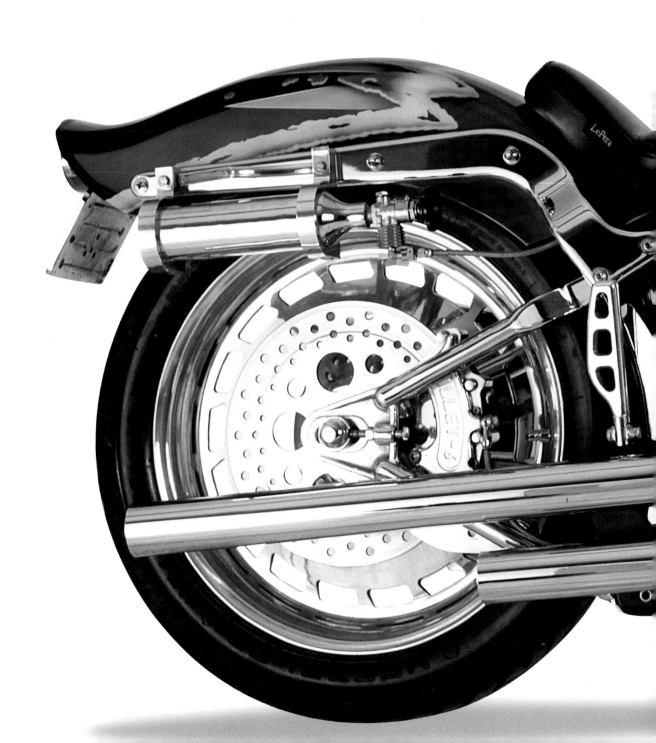

The engine has been fitted with a number of billet aluminium accessories including the primary drive cover seen here. Billet parts are very much a part of 90s custom-bike building.

To enhance the sleek lines the fuel tank has been lengthened into a graceful curve. The handlebars feature custom parts including master cylinders, grips and rear-view mirror.

Upside-down forks are where the lower fork tubes slide inside the upper tube; traditional forks are the other way round. Massive brake discs and calipers provide the stopping power.

SPECIFICATION

1995 Custom Lowrider Evo

Owner:	O.I.T.
	Breda, Holland

ENGINE

Model:	Evolution
Capacity:	80 cu in (1340 cc)
Cases:	HD
Carb:	S&S
Air filter:	Billet aluminium
Ignition:	Accel coils
Pipes:	custom drag

TRANSMISSION

Type:	five speed

FRAME

Model:	HD Softail modified to fit swingarm

SUSPENSION

Front:	telescopic forks
Rear:	monoshock

WHEELS AND BRAKES

Front:	19 in (48 cm) spoke
Brake:	twin discs
Rear:	16 in (41 cm) spoke
Brake:	disc

FENDERS

Front:	custom sport
Rear:	custom modified

ACCESSORIES

Handlebars:	dresser
Risers:	none
Headlight:	custom sealed beam
Tail-light:	cat's eye
Clocks:	tank-mounted dash
Tank:	modified Fatbob
Oil tank:	chromed horseshoe
Seat:	custom solo
Footrests:	billet forward controls
Electrics:	12-volt

PAINT AND FINISH

Paint:	custom
Colour:	one-off graphics
Chrome/polish:	billet aluminium

1991 Indian-Fendered Evolution

This gives an idea of what an Indian Chief bike might have looked like had the company survived, but this is a luxury custom bike on its own merit.

In building this model, considerable care has been taken to ensure that all the curves flow together throughout the length of the motorcycle.

This has been further enhanced through the two-tone paint scheme, with a third colour – chosen to complement the vintage badges – used for the pinstripe.

1956 Boothill Panhead

Bobbers that retained the stock two-piece Harley tanks, such as this motorcycle, were referred to as 'fatbobs' and, like many slang expressions, the term was widely used and became generally accepted.

Flames painted on the tank are another traditional custom touch. They flow down the lines of the tank and imply both motion and the fact that this is one hot motorcycle – many bobbers featured finely tuned engines for increased performance.

This bike is stroked to 86 cu in (1409 cc) through use of big twin flathead flywheels, but retains the standard bore and 1963 cylinder heads. It has been upgraded to 12-volt electrics and uses a later front end.

Evo

Indian-Fendered

Indian Motorcycles of Springfield, Massachusetts were Harley-Davidson's last domestic US competitor, but went out of business in 1953. One motorcycle they made was the Indian Chief, an opulent machine that featured hugely valanced fenders. Some contemporary custom bike builders have taken the idea of such fenders and applied them to Harley-Davidsons.

Flames are a traditional custom paint job, with endless variations in colour and shape. The gear shift knob is a miniature skull; pool balls and door knobs are also often used.

This Panhead engine is referred to as a stroker because its displacement has been increased through increasing the stroke (ie the distance the pistons move up and down).

The front drum brake has been enhanced by the fitment of an aluminium trim ring which assists in cooling the brake drum and eliminating the chance of brake fade.

SPECIFICATION

1956 Boothill Panhead

Owner:	Martin Henderson
	Farringdon, England

ENGINE

Model:	Panhead
Capacity:	86 cu in (1409 cc)
Cases:	HD
Carb:	S&S Super B
Air filter:	knuckle
Ignition:	points
Pipes:	two-into-one fishtail muffler

TRANSMISSION

Type:	four speed

FRAME

Model:	rigid Hydra Glide

SUSPENSION

Front:	telescopic forks
Rear:	none

WHEELS AND BRAKES

Front:	16 in (41 cm) spoked
Brake:	drum
Rear:	16 in (41 cm) spoked
Brake:	drum

FENDERS

Front:	FL modified
Rear:	FL modified

ACCESSORIES

Handlebars:	flat
Risers:	yes
Headlight:	9 in (23 cm)
Tail-light:	cat's eye
Clocks:	tank-mounted speedo
Tank:	Fatbob
Oil tank:	chromed horseshoe
Seat:	solo saddle
Footrests:	footboards
Electrics:	12-volt

PAINT AND FINISH

Paint:	Arthur Slade Boothill Motorcycles
Colour:	custom flames/black base
Chrome/polish:	chromed engine parts

Boothill Panhe

This Panhead is a modern version of the traditional bobber. In the ea
of custom-bike building, bikes were 'bobbed' by reducing the size of
and rear fenders and in many cases fitting a smaller gas tank such a
from a Mustang moped.

The air cleaner has been specifically made so that its overall shape mirrors the curves throughout the fenders and tank. It has been painted to further enhance this.

The stock Harley-Davidson gas tank has been lengthened so that it curves down into the solo saddle. The stock dash has been retained but a whiskey label now acts as the speedo face.

The single leather saddlebag was cut from cardboard templates and, like other components, designed so that its shape would reflect the rest of the machine.

SPECIFICATION

1991 Indian-Fendered Evolution

Owner:	Danny Fransen
	Genk, Belgium

ENGINE

Model:	Evolution
Capacity:	80 cu in (1340 cc)
Cases:	HD
Carb:	HD
Air filter:	custom-made
Ignition:	electronic
Pipes:	custom straight

TRANSMISSION

Type:	five speed

FRAME

Model:	Softail stock modified

SUSPENSION

Front:	telescopic forks
Rear:	none

WHEELS AND BRAKES

Front:	16 in (41 cm) cast alloy
Brake:	single disc
Rear:	16 in (41 cm) cast alloy
Brake:	disc

FENDERS

Front:	Indian Chief style
Rear:	Indian Chief style

ACCESSORIES

Handlebars:	flat
Risers:	none
Headlight:	custom sealed beam
Tail-light:	in saddlebag
Clocks:	tank-mounted dash
Tank:	modified stock
Oil tank:	horseshoe
Seat:	custom solo saddle
Footrests:	footboards
Electrics:	12-volt

PAINT AND FINISH

Paint:	custom
Colour:	black/silver
Chrome/polish:	minimal